The Price of Progress

Reconfiguring American Political History

Ronald P. Formisano, Paul Bourke, Donald DeBats, and Paula M. Baker

SERIES FOUNDERS

The Price of Progress

PUBLIC SERVICES, TAXATION,

AND THE AMERICAN CORPORATE STATE,

1877 TO 1929

R. RUDY HIGGENS-EVENSON

The Johns Hopkins University Press | BALTIMORE AND LONDON

© 2003 The Johns Hopkins University Press
All rights reserved. Published 2003
Printed in the United States of America on acid-free paper
2 4 6 8 9 7 5 3 1
The Johns Hopkins University Press
2715 North Charles Street
Baltimore, Maryland 21218-4363
www.press.jhu.edu

Library of Congress Cataloging-in-Publication Data

Higgens-Evenson, R. Rudy (Ronald Rudy), 1969–
The price of progress : public services, taxation, and the American
corporate state, 1877 to 1929 / R. Rudy Higgens-Evenson.
p. cm — (Reconfiguring American political history)
Includes bibliographical references and index.
ISBN 0-8018-7054-2 (hardcover : alk. paper)
1. Government spending policy—United States—States.
2. Taxation—United States—History—States. 3. Corporate
state—United States—History. 4. United States—Politics and
government. 5. United States—Economic conditions.
I. Title. II. Series
HJ20534.A1 H54 2002
336.73′09′034—dc21   2002001844

A catalog record for this book is available from the British Library.

To my brother and sister, Fred and Marty

CONTENTS

ACKNOWLEDGMENTS

I could not have written this book without the support of many people and agencies. University of Oregon College of Arts and Sciences Distinguished Professor James C. Mohr has made the transition with me from graduate advisor to colleague and friend. His unwavering support and encouragement for this project supported me when my own enthusiasm failed. Whatever contribution this book may make to the field originated in his graduate seminar on state government. He deserves credit for the best parts of this book. Its errors remain my own.

The patience and compassion of Robert J. Brugger, my editor at the Johns Hopkins University Press, allowed me to complete this book despite numerous delays attendant on a period of personal bereavement. His editorial advice provided an unwavering guide in honing the manuscript to a point. The insightful commentary of the Press's anonymous reader also helped focus my evidence significantly.

The support, understanding, and companionship of my fellow civil servants at the Office of Special Park Uses, Golden Gate National Recreation Area, have helped me through some of the roughest times of managing a full-time job and a scholarly manuscript. Greg Shine and Melinda Moses in particular have frequently rescued my morale.

Earlier versions of chapters 4 and 6 appeared in article form in *Social Science History* 26, no. 4 (winter 2002). A different part of chapter 4 was presented as a panel paper at the 1998 meeting of the American Historical Association. My fellow panelists—William Graebner, Colin Gordon, Colleen Dunlavy, and especially Ballard Campbell—all provided valuable feedback on my ideas.

Cathleen Leue, director of the University of Oregon Data Services Lab and Social Science Instructional Lab, contributed important institutional resources to the basic quantitative research behind this project. My research assistants,

Kerry Delf and Jill Griffen, did yeoman service in transcribing more state controller's reports than anyone should ever have to read. Many of those documents were procured through the prompt attention of Michelle Batchelor in the University of Oregon Knight Library Interlibrary Loan Department.

Several librarians and archivists helped me make good use of the resources of their institutions. In particular, Alyson Reichgott and Jennifer Tolpa showed me around the Massachusetts Historical Society. Sean Fisher, Massachusetts Metropolitan District Archivist, led me through an outstanding finding aid he devised for the papers of the Metropolitan Water and Sewer Commission and put me in touch with the right people at the Massachusetts State Archives.

John Wallis of the University of Maryland generously shared research from the data set he collected with Richard Sylla and John Legler. Pat Winans and Fred Evenson provided research assistance at the University of Nevada Library and the Nevada State Archives.

Early research for this manuscript benefited from comments by my dissertation committee: Gerald Berk, Richard M. Brown, Jeffrey Ostler, and Daniel Pope. Barbara Welke and Louise Wade also made helpful suggestions at several crucial moments. Paula Baker encouraged me in useful directions early on in the project and contributed important suggestions during its revision.

This project was supported in part by an Andrew Mellon Fellowship from the Center for the Study of New England History at the Massachusetts Historical Society. Travel funds were also provided by a mini-grant from the New Jersey State Historical Commission.

The Price of Progress

Introduction

CORPORATE STATES AND JEFFERSONIAN REPUBLICS

Americans have always argued about what government should do in their lives. Two of the most contentious issues have been the powers of government to give and to take away. From the Boston Tea Party to the property tax revolts of the 1970s and 1990s, Americans have tried to limit government's ability to tax its citizens. From Thomas Jefferson's critique of Alexander Hamilton's *Report on Manufactures* to recent protests against the World Bank and the International Monetary Fund, Americans have deeply questioned the involvement of business and government in each other's affairs. On one hand, Americans have asked how much power government should have to confiscate private resources. On the other, they have asked what useful public services government should provide.

During the half-century from 1877 to 1929—between the end of Reconstruction and the onset of the Great Depression—a new order fundamentally altered the basic terms of that debate. That new order was the American corporate state. In the corporate state, government took on a whole range of functions in cooperation with the business community. The corporate state was a compromise designed to subsidize the costs of new city and state programs by taxing corporations. In exchange for the financial support of the business community, city and state governments had to adopt business methods of management to make their costs more acceptable to taxpaying business owners. The American corporate state originated in the cash nexus of business taxation, where activist government met corporate capitalism.

The corporate state did not rise up everywhere at once throughout the nation; nor did its advent settle basic disagreements over the purpose and power of American government. Although some state governments made compromises of which Alexander Hamilton would have approved, many others followed Thomas Jefferson's dictum of governing best by governing least. The former group of states took on staggering new tasks; the latter held back, offering only limited public services. By 1929, the nation was a patchwork of Hamiltonian and Jeffersonian states existing side by side. Knowing how and why a particular state took one path and not the other is fundamental to understanding the origins of the American corporate state.

The stories of particular states make sense only in the context of the period's larger trends. Between 1877 and 1929, business and government were both revolutionized. Business grew in scale and scope, while government took on new functions or, in some cases, revived old ones. In the business world, firms used new techniques of manufacturing, transportation, and management to achieve unprecedented physical size and financial power. In government, the range of activities and the identity of decision makers changed radically. State and federal officials developed new business regulations, and city and state governments began to offer a wide variety of new public services. With the introduction of the initiative and the referendum, government decision making shifted away from legislators and toward the voters themselves, who by 1929 included women as well as men.

Of all the changes in late-nineteenth-century American business, the rise of the transcontinental railroad was the most epochal.[1] Not only did those huge new firms establish business practices that would form the foundation for a new industrial economy; their relationship with federal, state, and local governments also established (or reestablished) critical trends in regulation, taxation, and public investment in transportation. In terms of business practices, railroads introduced three critical innovations: widespread securities trading, high-speed transcontinental transportation, and management techniques that were capable of organizing the efforts of thousands of workers nationwide.

Although American investors had bought and sold stocks since the nation began, the railroads' endless demand for capital created the modern stock market. A reliable capital market was crucial for the growth of American corporations in the late nineteenth century. The explosion in stock and bond trading also created opportunities in finance for men such as John Pierpont Morgan, who could broker deals between European capitalists and American railroads and make a fortune in the process. The railroads and banking houses thrived as Americans and Europeans sank millions of dollars into the new enterprises.

The growth of an American capital market also was an important factor in changing old methods of taxation. The increasing concentration of American wealth in intangible forms such as stocks and bonds made it extremely difficult for tax collectors to accurately assess the nation's true resources. The obviously unfair balance of taxes paid by easily assessed owners of real estate, mostly farmers, and taxes paid by capitalists and investors, who could hide their stock certificates and bonds, became one of the major political pressures for tax reform between 1877 and 1929.

Cross-country transportation and communication created the infrastructure that was necessary for a variety of other industries that relied on nationwide markets. Anything that could be sold, from wheat to sewing machines, could enter markets anywhere in the nation. Telegraph wires followed railroad lines, so instantaneous communication spread across the country as well. Any information, from stock quotes to personnel actions, could be sent from coast to coast.

As the nation's first big businesses, railroads also pioneered in management techniques. Employing thousands of workers and millions of dollars' worth of locomotives, rolling stock, buildings, land, and equipment, they required a whole new method of doing business. Timetables required coordination among offices scattered across the entire country. Railroad managers developed new administrative techniques for managing their vast enterprises, including the modern division between "line" and "staff" personnel.

In terms of their relationship to the government, railroads marked a return to a policy of "internal improvements," or government subsidy of transportation projects. From 1812 to the late 1830s, the federal government and the states had engaged in a variety of internal improvement projects, including the federal government's National Road and the state of New York's Erie Canal. Following the Depression of 1837, however, federal and state governments pulled back sharply from internal improvements. Only during the Civil War did the federal government reinvest in internal improvements. Congress granted federal charters, vast tracts of land, and huge loans to several firms that promised to build transcontinental railroads. In 1869, two of those companies—the Union Pacific, building westward from Omaha, and the Central

Pacific, building eastward from Sacramento—linked their rails with a ceremonial golden spike at Promontory Point, Utah.

Counties and towns joined the federal government in railroad fever. Localities offered loans and land grants to various railroads throughout the 1870s and 1880s in attempts to lure economic development. In many cases, towns went into debt to offer railroads financial incentives to build. By the turn of the twentieth century, those debts had become a significant element of local finance and a sore point during annual tax levies.

The railroads' methods of finance and management became models for other enterprises that took advantage of new economies of scale to expand dramatically. Along with the railroads came various communication and transportation firms. The most prominent were the so-called express companies, such as Wells Fargo, which were essentially shipping contractors for the railroads. Communications firms such as American Telegraph and Telephone, which operated wires alongside the railroad tracks, kept pace with the railroads' rapid growth.

Other industries also found that bigger was better. In chemical refining and steel manufacturing, for example, technological innovations made possible mass production of large batches. Manufacturers soon found that the only limits to their ability to produce were their supply and distribution systems. To solve those problems, firms such as Standard Oil, Carnegie Steel, and DuPont Chemicals integrated vertically, by buying up their suppliers and distributors, as well as horizontally, by buying up their competitors.

Extreme economic cycles also contributed to corporate consolidation in the late nineteenth and early twentieth centuries. Depressions in 1873, 1893, and 1907 presented opportunities for well-positioned firms to buy out their weaker competitors and increase market share. In each round, the biggest businesses got even bigger. In 1901, for example, J. P. Morgan bought Carnegie Steel from Andrew Carnegie to create US Steel, thereby creating the nation's first billion-dollar firm.

New developments in government regulation, especially at the federal level, also contributed to the rise of big business. Those regulations resulted from decades of political agitation, beginning in the 1870s. Since the administration of President Andrew Jackson in the 1830s, many Americans—especially farmers, laborers, and small businessmen—harbored deep suspicions of any large aggregation of capital. They suspected the young industrial titans of corrupting Congress and the state legislatures. They blamed the railroads in particular for the depression of 1873, not entirely without reason. Between 1874 and

1877, several midwestern states enacted "Granger Laws" that demonstrated just how much trouble state legislatures could make for big business. Named for the farmers' organizations that sponsored them, the new regulations restricted railroad freight rates and business practices. From the railroads' perspective, the problem was not that the laws were unreasonable but that they varied from state to state and could be changed at every biennial meeting of the legislature. After a decade of U.S. Supreme Court decisions and congressional haggling, the Interstate Commerce Commission Act of 1886 created a federal agency to which railroads could appeal from the unpredictable regulations of the states.[2]

The political status of corporations remained controversial for the next quarter-century. The new competitive tactics made possible by sheer size, such as Standard Oil's ability to strangle regional competitors by slashing prices in particular regions, provoked protests from smaller businesses. The result was the Sherman Anti-Trust Act of 1890. The Sherman Act actually contributed to the growth of large firms in the 1890s by prohibiting cooperative arrangements among smaller companies. Barred from "anti-competitive" arrangements such as tying contracts or holding trusts, large firms simply bought their smaller competitors outright.[3]

The early 1890s also witnessed the rise of one of the most radically anti-corporate political parties in American history: the People's Party, or Populists. Their famous Omaha Platform of 1892 demanded government ownership of all utilities, including railroads, telegraphs, and telephones. They sought structural reforms as well, including women's suffrage and approval or revocation of specific laws in popular elections by means of the initiative and referendum. In 1896, they endorsed Democratic presidential candidate William Jennings Bryan. When Bryan lost, the Populist movement disintegrated.

After the turn of the twentieth century, big business faced a different political challenge in the Progressive movement. Where the Populists had forced the corporations to fight for their very existence, the Progressives sought only to control corporate behavior. Led in part by business officials seeking détente with disgruntled consumers and voters, the Progressive movement sought to legitimize big business by regulating it. Some Progressives, such as President Theodore Roosevelt, actually encouraged "good" monopolies that could pass on their economies of scale to the consumer. Others, such as President Woodrow Wilson, continued the approach of the Sherman Act, attempting to foster small business by restraining the anticompetitive practices of large corporations. In 1914, the Federal Trade Commission (FTC) Act and the Clayton

Act finally legitimized big business by requiring firms to make regular public reports on profit and loss, satisfying most Progressives' demands for regulatory measures.[4]

In the same year that Congress passed the FTC and Clayton Acts, Henry Ford started up the world's first mechanized assembly line at his plant in Highland Park, Michigan. Ford's technique allowed him to manufacture automobiles with a speed and efficiency that made them affordable for ordinary consumers. Just as the transcontinental railroad had been the driving engine of transformation for American business in the late nineteenth century, the automobile revolutionized American business in the early twentieth century. Where the scope and scale of the railroads had been a new thing under the sun, however, Ford was only refining existing ideas and techniques. In 1911, for example, the famous industrial engineer Frederick W. Taylor had already articulated what he called "the principles of scientific management" for improving employee productivity by means of time and motion studies in manufacturing.[5] Nevertheless, the automobile industry in general was revolutionary because it created vast new demand in whole industries, including glass, rubber, steel, and refined petroleum products.

The same year that Congress passed the FTC Act and Ford opened his plant in Highland Park, Archduke Franz Ferdinand, heir to the throne of Austro-Hungaria, was assassinated in Sarajevo. Various governments invoked alliances among the great powers of Europe, drawing the continent into the first World War. Overseas demand for chemicals, steel, and other materiel brought windfall profits to American industry. In 1917, the United States officially entered the conflict. The war changed American business and politics forever. The federal government took control of the railroads and imposed heavy taxes on industries that profited from the war. In politics, dissident groups such as the Socialist Party, which had became a significant force during the 1910s, dissolved or went underground in the wake of anticommunist hysteria attendant on the Russian Revolution of 1917.

After the war ended in 1919, Americans rushed back to normalcy. The federal government immediately released its grip on the railroads and started reducing the war profits tax. In politics, the balance between business and reformers had reversed. Where businessmen had struggled to placate or defeat reform politicians between 1877 and 1914, politicians did their best to imitate businessmen between 1919 and 1929. President Calvin Coolidge declared that the business of America was business. As inflation became a significant economic force for the first time since the Civil War, Americans grew preoccupied with the high cost of living. Now, instead of promising to topple big business, campaigning politicians promised prosperity, business methods in government, and electric washing machines for everyone.

The mechanics of electoral politics changed as much as their content. During the 1910s, Progressive reformers had introduced several reforms, including open primaries, the initiative and the referendum, and women's suffrage. By the 1920s, women voted in all elections, and many Americans found themselves voting directly for laws that had previously been considered only by state legislatures. Interest groups began to replace political parties as the organizing powers behind electoral politics. The carnival atmosphere of late-nineteenth-century electioneering shifted toward more businesslike public relations campaigns for people and measures. Voter participation declined.

In this larger context of revolutionary change in business and politics between 1877 and 1929, the American corporate state was created. The "corporate state, American style" stood apart from other corporatist governments that arose worldwide during the early twentieth century.[6] Politically, American corporatism lacked the totalitarian ideology and blunt coercion of fascist governments such as the world's first self-styled modern corporate state, Benito Mussolini's Italy. Economically, American government lacked direct control of production and pricing, and American business lacked true cartels or even cohesive voluntary associations.[7] Nevertheless, the phrase "corporate state" accurately distinguished the new order of business-government relations in the United States from what had gone before.[8]

Our present understanding of the origins of the American corporate state consists mainly of historical work on the activities of the federal government, and for good reason. Federal antitrust policy established the political legitimacy of corporate capitalism. Even though the federal government regulated interstate commerce, however, individual commonwealths still governed the conduct of business within their own borders. As contemporary British observer James Bryce put it, "If one regards the sphere of its action and the completeness of its control in that sphere," including "the supervision of all local governments, and unlimited power of taxation," the authority of the state was "vast."[9] Firms doing business in single states—particularly urban utilities such as street railways, telephone, and gas companies—had a vested interest in how states regulated their business. If corporate taxes began to bite into their profits, they immediately demanded to be allowed to charge the public higher rates or, alternatively, tried to outlaw their competitors on the grounds that such competition would diminish their profits and hence the state's revenues. Federal policy was undeniably significant in the legitimization of corporate capitalism, but state-level policy was equally important in building up the corporate state.

In fact, the real innovations in American government between Reconstruction and the New Deal came at the city and state level.[10] Some of the most important departures, which set new terms for old debates over the government's power to give and take away, consisted of expensive new public services and the new business taxes that paid for them.

Three basic projects accounted for most of the growth in government activity during the period: infrastructure, education, and public welfare. Vast municipal utility projects laid the foundations, literally as well as figuratively, for twentieth-century urban development. To finance their new water, power, and sewer systems, cities had to turn to state governments for new powers to borrow and tax. At the state level, grading far-flung rural highways tested the financial and administrative resources of even the wealthiest and most sophisticated state governments. Public education, the period's most expensive public service, absorbed a complex mix of city, county, and state funding, with the states taking over a larger share as time went by. A jumble of disparate institutions—including widows' and orphans' homes, poor houses, and state insane asylums (lumped together under the heading of "charities and corrections" in 1877)—by 1929 had developed into systems of schools for the handicapped and psychiatric hospitals under the centralized supervision of state departments of public welfare.

Many Americans summed up those new projects with the term "progress." The precise political meaning of the word remained vague through the mid-1920s,[11] despite the fact that in 1912 the Progressive Party had launched one of the most significant third-party presidential bids in American history. For many contemporaries, as for us, "progress" simply meant government's assumption of new functions or services.[12] New functions required more revenue. More revenue required tax reform. Tax reform often meant the corporation tax, as well as the new style of politics and administration that went with it. The price of progress was more than just the corporation tax; it was the invention of the corporate state itself.

The old property tax failed to touch the wealthiest Americans' growing investments in corporate stock and bonds. Several states solved that problem by imposing new taxes on corporate property and incomes. In 1913, the Sixteenth Amendment to the U.S. Constitution authorized the federal government to levy a personal income tax, which followed the example established by several states—most notably Wisconsin. Until the Great Depression struck in 1929, however, the vast majority of income taxes were paid by corporations and very wealthy individuals. Only the deep pockets of the corporations could support the new functions undertaken by state and city governments.

Big business tended to support the new taxes because the new corporation taxes usually were administered at the state level and often included some kind of relief from local taxation. State-level taxation also meant standardization of costs. Instead of a multitude of local assessments and rates, businesses could pay a single state rate with a more or less predictable assessment. Most states also held extensive hearings before enacting such taxes, allowing business officials significant influence on how heavy to make the tax and which sectors should bear the heaviest burdens.

Rising business tax rates gave corporation officials an incentive to get involved in the affairs of state and municipal government. Business officials took a new interest in the conduct of government affairs as a long-term investment in controlling costs. Private nonprofit organizations, including bureaus of municipal research and taxpayers' associations, helped state and municipal governments adopt business methods, which usually meant consolidating department functions, standardizing job descriptions and payrolls, and centralizing purchasing and personnel. The most important new business method was the executive budget. The executive budget placed the responsibility for all spending proposals with the city or state executive, leaving the city council or legislature only the power to approve or disapprove. Government began to look more and more like business. By 1929, the rise of the corporate state had fundamentally changed the relationship between government and business. Business officials had gone from bribing and blackmailing state legislators to helping them run government on a paying basis. For their part, state officials had abandoned their biennial attempts to soak the corporations and instead asked them to set their own tax rates.

Such was the situation in corporate states such as New York, New Jersey, Pennsylvania, Massachusetts, Wisconsin, and California, where corporation taxes funded new public services in a cooperative arrangement between business and government along the lines laid out by Alexander Hamilton in the 1790s. Hamilton's ideas seemed to embody the spirit of the age. In fact, Progressives such as President Theodore Roosevelt, Secretary of State Elihu Root, and Columbia University president Nicholas Murray Butler self-consciously identified themselves as followers of Alexander Hamilton.[13] Massachusetts Senator Henry Cabot Lodge even wrote a biography of Hamilton. New York

Bureau of Municipal Research promoter Luther Gulick pointed to Hamilton's *Federalist* 72 as the origin of the concept of the executive budget in America.[14]

On the other hand, states such as Michigan, Illinois, Kansas, Nebraska, Mississippi, Alabama, the Dakotas, Oregon, and Nevada made their way into the twentieth century guided by political ideas that were more in line with those of Thomas Jefferson. Those states focused authority at the county and municipal level, limiting the state's authority and responsibilities. Few of those states adopted corporation taxes, and none relied heavily on them. Among them only Illinois reorganized its state government to adopt business methods of administration. Jefferson's name was rarely invoked to justify those states' adherence to local government, property taxation, and minimal state-level services. When Progressive writers such as Herbert Croly mentioned Jefferson, usually it was to declare that the new methods of government were using "Hamiltonian means" to accomplish "Jeffersonian ends."[15] The term "Jeffersonian republic" might have sounded somewhat strange to contemporaries, but its connotations of agrarianism, local government, and suspicion of government power make it a useful category for the analysis that follows.

Three basic factors—economy, institutional structure, and political contingency—determined the course of institutional change in each state. Each state's mix of agriculture and industry established the conditions under which utilities, manufacturers, or bankers rose to political power. The structure of the state itself also played an important part in making a state corporate or Jeffersonian. In the persons of various state officials—especially experts in medicine, education, and engineering—state governments exerted a surprising influence over their own destinies. Historians and political scientists of the school generally known as "new institutionalist" already have applied this idea to the federal government.[16] As one historian already has shown, new institutionalism offers significant insight into the comparative development of the individual states as well.[17] Not only did state officials and their agencies play important roles in political change, but the structural distribution of authority between state and local governments also mattered a great deal in setting a particular state on a Hamiltonian or Jeffersonian path.

The other factor in the rise of the corporate state was political contingency. American political scientists invented the notion of pluralism in the early twentieth century to describe the phenomenon of interest-group politics.[18] Although political scientists have largely abandoned this notion, some historians of the period have revived it with significant results.[19] Each state's turn toward corporatism or Jeffersonianism depended on its own mix of interest groups, political parties, individual firms, and their reactions to political events of the day. Those political events could range from a shift in the balance of power between the two major parties to a widely publicized scandal involving corporate tax evasion or substandard conditions in mental hospitals. Aside from the broader, social-scientific trends of state economies and institutional structure, the purely historical accidents of political opportunism also played an important role in creating the corporate state.

Contemporary economists and officials often complained about the "considerable diversity" in the states' methods of business taxation.[20] For outsiders looking in, however, as James Bryce noted, differences could be instructive; Bryce considered "the financial systems in force in the several States . . . one of the widest and most instructive fields of study that the whole range of American institutions presents."[21] In fact, he wished that "some person equipped with the necessary special knowledge could survey them with a philosophic eye, and present the results of his survey in a concise form."[22] The brief survey that follows applies the comparative method to state revenues and expenditures to explore why some states became corporate and some became Jeffersonian.[23]

Compromise, Corruption, and Confrontation

TAX REFORM IN THE 1870S

The crisis of the property tax began in the economic and political maelstrom of the 1870s. Many Americans blamed the decade's economic turmoil—including a stock market crash, a severe depression, and violent railroad strikes—on the misdeeds of big money. The Panic of 1873, for example, started when banker Jay Cooke failed to sell millions of dollars' worth of Northern Pacific Railroad bonds. Having bought the bonds from the railroad with borrowed money, he found himself unable to repay his creditors. He plunged into bankruptcy and dragged them down with him. The financial disaster sent shock waves through the entire economy, resulting in a downturn that would be known until the 1930s as the Great Depression. Simultaneously, the federal government quietly ceased minting money from silver. In a decade when new silver bonanzas in the West made the metal cheap and plentiful, that decision contributed to deflation and made money harder to borrow. Quickly labeled "the Crime of '73" by farmers and labor groups, the end of silver coinage was widely interpreted as the government's commitment to helping bankers instead of debtors and workers.[1]

The Great Strike of 1877 exemplified the worst that could happen in the decade's confrontation between labor and capital. On July 17, 1877, at Martinsburg, West Virginia, trainmen on the Baltimore and Ohio Railroad protesting layoffs combined with a 10 percent wage cut stopped working and refused to let trains leave the station. Militiamen were called out in Baltimore, but crowds refused to let their trains leave and set the station on fire. In Pittsburgh, where the strike spread to the Pennsylvania Railroad, the militia refused to organize; when militiamen from Philadelphia arrived, they had to fight a pitched battle against townspeople who pinned them down in the train station and then burned it to the ground. By the end of the strike, more than ninety people, mostly strikers, had been killed.[2]

Electoral politics seemed to be unable to provide any answers. Bribery scandals discredited both major parties. In 1871, the *New York Times* revealed that New York City's Democratic administration, including mayor A. Oakley Hall and commissioner of public works William M. "Boss" Tweed, had been manipulating huge municipal contracts for their own profit. The name Boss Tweed became synonymous with corruption in city government. In 1873, Mark Twain and Charles Dudley Warner published *The Gilded Age*, a novel lampooning the self-serving projects of contemporary politicians. The book's popularity underscored many Americans' belief that government officials cared more about making a buck than representing their constituents.[3] In 1876, Republican president Ulysses S. Grant's private secretary, Orville H. Babcock, and secretary of war William Belknap both resigned amid scandal. Babcock had grown rich by helping whiskey manufacturers evade excise taxes, and Belknap had been caught taking bribes from Indian agents.

The ultimate political disappointment of the decade, at least for northerners who had sacrificed so much to win the Civil War, was the so-called Compromise of 1877. This compromise was an agreement by which the contested presidential election of 1876 was awarded to Republican Rutherford B. Hayes in exchange for the withdrawal of federal troops from the South.[4] With the military gone, no one was left to enforce the civil and political rights of the ex-slaves. All-white "Redeemer" state governments quickly replaced Reconstruction administrations throughout the South. The Compromise of 1877 unraveled America's greatest experiment in racial equality.

Among the economic disasters and political disillusionment of the 1870s, many Americans would have numbered the everyday injustices of their tax system.[5] The general property tax ripped off farmers while pampering rich investors. It fell heaviest on land, buildings, and livestock but barely touched stocks and bonds—the bulk of America's new corporate wealth. Both forms of property, the physical and the intangible, supposedly paid the same rate of taxation. But the locally elected, part-time assessors who actually collected the tax lacked not only the know-how but also the inclination to assess stocks and bonds because energetic assessment meant unpopularity and defeat in the next election. As Jay Cooke's Northern Pacific debacle and the ensuing Panic of 1873 showed, stocks and bonds were growing increasingly important to the American economy. Nevertheless, they remained practically tax exempt because they were so easy to hide. In a depression that already pitted farmers against railroads, the outdated and poorly administered property tax exacerbated the decade's worst economic tensions.

Under the property tax system as it was actually enforced, the only forms of corporate wealth that were subject to taxation were real estate and tangible personal property. County assessors who were unable to track down stocks and bonds had no trouble finding railroad tracks, plots of land, buildings, and equipment. Corporate property tax assessments usually came in much too high or much too low, depending on whether the property was in a rural county far from corporate headquarters or in an urban county, where politically powerful officials at company headquarters could influence assessments. In rural counties, assessors who went easy on farm and residential property soaked corporate real estate and equipment for all they were worth. The corporations, after all, did not live there and could not vote them out of office. On the other hand, in urban counties where the corporations wielded political clout, assessors had to lowball corporate valuations if they wanted to stay in office. Faced with a different tax bill in every county, business officials found the situation intolerable. So did farmers, legislators, and state financial officials.

New England and Middle Atlantic states hit on the corporation tax as a compromise that would address the concerns of state government, business, and local government. State governments would levy a new tax on corporations on the basis of the value of stock or earnings or both. In exchange for paying a new tax to the state, corporations would get relief from local taxes. Because local tax rates usually were five to ten times higher than state tax rates, and local assessments could be unpredictably high, businesses often welcomed state corporation taxes. In exchange for losing a valuable part of their tax base, local governments would get some of the revenue from the new corporation tax. Individual taxpayers also would see reductions in their total taxes because corporation taxes would replace state-level property taxation.

Financial enterprises were the first type of business to become subject to special taxes. Early taxation of banks and insurance companies went hand-in-hand with regulation of those enterprises. Pennsylvania, for example, levied a tax on bank stock dividends as early as 1824, supposedly taxing net profits at the source.[6] In practice, however, officials generally ignored the law and neglected to collect the tax.[7] The same year that Pennsylvania passed its tax on bank stock, New York levied a tax on insurance premiums, based on gross receipts.[8] In both cases, the states imposed taxes as part of legislative packages that included regulations on how financial companies did business. By the 1870s, most states levied some sort of taxes on banks and insurance companies as part of their regulatory regime.

In 1844, Pennsylvania enacted the first true general corporation tax. In one form or another, it remained in force into the 1910s.[9] What made the new tax so innovative was its broad authority. It applied to all businesses organized as corporations, except for financial companies, which the state already taxed under the law of 1824. The 1844 law required corporations to pay a state tax that was based on the actual value of their capital stock. The act also exempted from local taxation all corporate property that was directly involved in the corporation's main business, as well as stocks and bonds.[10] So although the corporations had to pay a new tax to the state, they no longer had to suffer the slings and arrows of a thousand local valuations, nor did they have to pay the higher local property tax rate. The state got a new source of revenue, and corporations got relief from local taxation. Individual taxpayers were freed from state property taxes because the new corporation tax generated enough revenue to pay the expenses of state government. Only the localities were left out; they got nothing to replace the corporate property that the state tax removed from their tax bases.

Not until the horror of the Civil War two decades later would another state follow Pennsylvania in imposing a general corporation tax. In 1864, Massachusetts enacted a corporation tax as a war measure.[11] Unlike the Pennsylvania corporation tax, the Massachusetts tax split corporation tax revenues between the state and localities. The Pennsylvania corporation tax allowed localities to tax only corporate property that was not directly involved in the main business of the firm. For example, a Pennsylvania county could tax vacant lots owned by a railroad but not tracks, depots, or locomotives. In contrast, Massachusetts counties could tax any physical property owned by corporations, railroad tracks and all.

Massachusetts redistributed proceeds of the corporation tax among the towns on the basis of stockholder residence. The more stockholders a town had, the more money it got. The state retained only tax revenue that was proportionate to the stock owned by out-of-state investors, which amounted to about a quarter of the total receipts of the corporation tax. Thus, the corporation tax created a massive and somewhat lopsided system of intergovernmental payments in Massachusetts because the dozen or so towns that had most of the state's wealth ended up with most of the redistributed corporation tax revenue.

The Massachusetts corporation tax benefited farmers and big-city taxpayers. Farmers' state tax burden was lightened by the new source of state revenue, and city dwellers' municipal tax burden was alleviated by the new transfer payments to the towns. Furthermore, corporate capital in the form of stocks now bore a larger share of the cost of government. In contrast to New York and California, where corporate taxation provoked years of litigation, in Massachusetts "little complaint is heard regarding these taxes," according to a later tax commission's report, because the "burdens" of the tax were "steady, regular, predictable," allowing taxpayers "to make calculations and adjust their affairs" accordingly.[12]

What made the Massachusetts and Pennsylvania taxes unique in the United States was the fact that they touched corporate capital at all. In both states, the new corporation taxes required company treasurers to report the value of corporate stock to state officials. In Pennsylvania, firms paid a tax that was based on the total value of the firm's stock. In Massachusetts, firms paid a tax that was based on the value of the stock less the amount of physical property taxed by the localities. That difference between the firm's intangible value, expressed as the total worth of its capital stock, and its tangible value, expressed as the value assessed by local assessors, was called the "corporate excess." So although Pennsylvania firms had to pay a larger state tax, their local tax burden was smaller because much of their property was exempt from local taxes. Massachusetts companies paid a smaller state tax because they were assessed only on the corporate excess, but their local tax liabilities were higher.

In Pennsylvania and Massachusetts, individual capitalists came out the real winners. Both states' corporation taxes effectively created a personal tax break for investors. Before the advent of the corporation tax, stocks had been assessed as the property of individual stockholders; afterward, they were assessed as the company's property. The benefit to individual stockholders therefore was proportionate to the amount of stock each owned; the more stock, the greater the tax break. But firms had to absorb the blow in the form of larger tax bills. In effect, the corporation tax transformed an existing (but poorly administered) tax on corporate capital from a personal liability into a business expense.

From the perspective of state officials, the corporation tax offered a more accurate and powerful method of touching corporate capital. Before the corporation tax, local assessors found it virtually impossible to accurately evaluate, let alone tax, corporate capital in the form of stocks and bonds in the hands of investors. The corporation tax allowed the state to use widely publicized information about the capitalization of large firms as a basis for assessing corporate capital. Thus, the corporation tax made the state's receipts from corporate capital much larger and more predictable.

The general assault on the property tax began in 1871.[13] In that year, the New York Tax Commission issued a landmark report condemning the Empire State's existing personal property tax on stocks and bonds as "a libel upon the intelligence and honesty of both those who enact and those who administer the laws."[14] The report was significant for two reasons. First, it was written by the most respected tax expert of the day, David Ames Wells, so tax officials from around the country took it seriously. Second, it articulated the problems of the general property tax and proposed business taxation as a solution.

David Wells served his literary and intellectual apprenticeship at the Springfield *Republican* in the late 1840s before moving on to New York City and working for G. P. Putnam and Sons as an editor in the 1850s. Like many reformers of the 1870s, Wells made his reputation during the Civil War. His contribution to the war effort consisted of a pamphlet titled *Our Burden and Our Strength*. Published in 1864, the pamphlet offered detailed statistical evidence for the credibility of the Union's claims that it would be able to redeem the war bonds that were such a vital part of its wartime finances. Thanks to that publication, Wells was appointed chairman of the United States Revenue Commission in 1865.

For the next five years, Wells was the nation's single most influential policymaker in federal taxation, serving as Special Commissioner of the Revenue until 1870. Wells's job was to administer the rudimentary federal income tax imposed during the Civil War, as well as tariffs and other duties collected by the federal government. Wells endeared himself to American businessmen by opposing all taxes on manufacturing and supporting a protective tariff, at least in his early reports. Although he remained opposed to taxing manufacturers throughout his career, he changed his mind on the tariff. Despite the fact that his crucial work on Ulysses Grant's presidential campaign had made him a frontrunner for secretary of the Treasury, Wells published a report in 1869 that he knew would probably end his government career. He had come to the conclusion that the protective tariff hurt American consumers—and said as much in his annual report. Although reformers from both parties praised the report, it ran counter to the Republican party line. Because Wells's report condemned the tariff, Republicans in Congress convinced President Grant to eliminate his position in 1870.[15]

When Wells joined the New York Tax Commission, he brought to bear on the question of state and local taxes his expertise and reputation as a nationally known tax official. In his analysis of New York's tax system, Wells made two recommendations for reform. First, he suggested that New York should abandon its attempt to tax intangible property, especially in light of New Jersey's 1869 law exempting stocks and bonds from taxation "in certain of the counties and cities of that State which lie contiguous to New York."[16] Second, Wells proposed that New York impose a tax on "all corporations created by the state which are in the nature of a monopoly," such as gas companies, banks, and railroads.[17] Although the New York legislature declined to adopt these recommendations, the Wells report was a landmark in the theory of business taxation.[18] It clearly articulated the idea that corporations should be taxed at the state level because their legal powers derived from special incorporating acts of the state legislature. It also called attention to the administrative weaknesses and real injustices of existing methods of taxing intangible property.

As Wells pointed out in the 1872 sequel to his report, such weaknesses were inherent in any tax system that attempted to assess stocks and bonds. Even Massachusetts, which exempted stocks of domestic corporations from local taxation, still had trouble assessing other kinds of corporate capital—especially bonds, which remained subject to taxation as the personal property of investors. In fact, Massachusetts legislators gave up trying to find the real value of stocks and bonds in the hands of investors and empowered local assessors to simply assign valuations. First, taxpayers had to submit a statement listing their personal property, including intangibles such as bonds and the stock of corporations from other states. Then, in a procedure known as "dooming," assessors met in secret and estimated the most likely amount of such property the person actually owned. The assessors usually marked up the amount originally reported by a factor of two or three in a system Wells dismissed as "inquisitorial, arbitrary and pagan."[19] Capitalists called the system "despotic," "monstrous," and "absurd," and even Massachusetts state officials admitted it involved some "guesswork."[20]

Even in the capital-starved South and West, officials bemoaned their inability to tap intangible wealth. In California, for example, mortgages were tax exempt until 1872.[21] Throughout the late 1870s, officials in Alabama repeatedly condemned low property valuations in the urban counties of Montgomery and Mobile for failing to account fully for the intangible forms of wealth that were accumulating there.[22] "Do not pursue private persons and swear them about the contents of their safes and their pockets," *The Nation* advised state officials at the end of the decade, "because it is both useless and productive of gross fraud and of a habit of contempt for the law."[23] Instead, the editors suggested, the states should go directly to the source and tax corporations.

Taxing the physical property of corporations posed problems of its own. Local assessors could not be trusted to evaluate the property of statewide firms with accuracy or fairness. During the depression year of 1873 in New York, for example, local assessors put the value of railroad property at anywhere from $325 to $26,000 per mile. "There is no uniform rule," complained the state board of assessors, "for any road, in any county, each assessor being governed entirely by his own views."[24] As the California controller put it in 1872, local assessors "are in many instances unacquainted with the value of this species of property [i.e. railroads], and are unduly subject to local influences and interests. The result of this is a great inequality of taxation."[25]

State officials and business managers thought the system gave too much autonomy to county assessors. State officials thought county assessors were too easily bribed or intimidated by corporate officials in urban counties. Corporate officials thought county assessors were too likely to inflate corporate property values out in the sticks, where it was popular to soak big business. In the 1870s, the problem was most severe with the railroads, and the decade's most significant tax reforms revolved around those enterprises.

Railroads were built with special taxes already attached. As early as 1832, for example, New Jersey granted a monopoly to the Camden and Amboy Railroad in exchange for a share of their profits large enough to sustain the state government.[26] In 1846, Michigan first taxed railroads on the basis of their total stock, as opposed to their physical property.[27] In 1854, Wisconsin made a classic corporate compromise by shifting the basis of railroad taxes to gross receipts and exempting the railroads from local taxation in exchange for a state license fee. The railroads themselves gave the measure their heartiest support.[28]

As philosopher Henry Adams put it at the end of the nineteenth century, "The generation between 1865 and 1895 was already mortgaged to the railways, and no one knew it better than the generation itself."[29] Under the pressure of rising railroad shipping rates, farmers and merchants in particular turned to politics as a way to defend their economic interests from what they regarded as predatory and monopolistic practices. The largest and best-known group among farmers was the Patrons of Husbandry, known as the Grange. Formed in the late 1860s, the Grange movement spread throughout the West. By the early 1870s, Grangers had become a significant third-party movement in many states.

In the Midwest, the railroad taxes of the 1870s coincided with Granger campaigns to regulate railroad shipping practices and rates.[30] Unlike the corporation taxes levied earlier by Pennsylvania and Massachusetts, most of the Granger railroad tax reforms of the 1870s only addressed problems of assessment; they refrained from imposing new state taxes on railroads. In 1872, for example, Illinois—a leading Granger state—adopted a new system of assessing railroad property. State officials would assess all railroad property that was directly involved in the company's main business—such as tracks, depots, and locomotives—and leave the remaining property to be assessed by local officials. The state board of equalization would then apportion the value of the property to each county, depending on the proportion of track that ran through the county. The localities would still tax all railroad property, even property assessed by the state; only the method of assessment changed. Illinois retained that system of state assessment through the first decade of the twentieth century.[31] In 1873, Michigan changed its methods of assessing railroad property from the capital-stock method to the gross-earnings method of taxing railroads, but without imposing any new taxes.[32] In 1876, Kansas followed suit by centralizing railroad assessments under the authority of a state board, as did Alabama a year later.[33] Because the new methods of assessment made tax assessments more predictable, the railroads often welcomed such reforms.

No region was friendlier to the railroads during the 1870s than the South. During and after Reconstruction, southern politicians tried a variety of fiscal incentives to bring those engines of economic development to their war-torn region. Land grants, loans, and direct railroad subsidies depleted the treasuries of southern states, and tax exemptions prevented the cash-strapped states from raising much-needed revenue from the nation's first big businesses.[34] Despite their vocal complaints about Republican corruption and railroad deals while they were out of office during Reconstruction, Democratic "Redeemers" merely continued the same policies of corporate tax breaks into the 1880s. Georgia made railroads liable to the same property taxes as individuals in 1874, and Mississippi imposed a small per-mile tax on railroads in 1875, though neither tax generated much revenue.[35]

The only state that attempted to impose significant new taxes on railroads in the 1870s quickly discovered how easily corporate resistance could kill tax reform. The California railroad tax revolt that began with the state constitutional convention of 1879 underscored all the weaknesses of the old property tax system. Informal side deals between county assessors and the railroad suddenly became grounds for lawsuits that went all the way to the U.S. Supreme Court. The railroad's refusal to pay its taxes disorganized county finances across the state. The entire controversy ultimately resulted in perhaps the most significant Supreme Court decision on the legal status of corporations in American history, *Santa Clara County v. Southern Pacific Railroad*.[36]

In the late 1870s, California underwent a major economic and political upheaval. The completion of the transcontinental railroad, the spreading aftershocks of the financial earthquake of 1873, and an extended drought resulted in widespread unemployment in the Golden State. In 1877, a former drayman named Denis Kearney organized the crowds of jobless workers loitering in the streets of San Francisco into the Workingmen's Party of California, or WPC.[37] At their first official meeting on October 5, 1877, members of the WPC resolved, "We propose to destroy the great money power of the rich by a system of taxation that will make great wealth impossible in the future."[38] Partly as a result of WPC agitation, a state constitutional convention was scheduled for 1879. The resulting document created a railroad commission with potentially sweeping regulatory powers and set new rules for corporate taxation. The radical potential of the California constitution of 1879 drew worldwide attention. New York legislators denounced it as "the most infamous Constitution ever forced upon a people."[39] The London *Times* compared its "absurd" and "menacing" provisions to the agenda of the Paris Commune.[40] Karl Marx himself wrote to a contemporary that California was "very important" to him "because nowhere else has the upheaval most shamelessly caused by capitalist centralization taken place with such speed."[41]

Although the California constitution of 1879 never fulfilled its most radical potential, its corporate taxation clause fundamentally rearranged the fiscal relationship among corporations, county government, and state government by imposing new taxes on corporate stocks and bonds. The constitution of 1879 specifically defined corporate franchises and corporate debt as property subject to taxation—a major departure from previous tax law in the Golden State.

Like the new railroad assessment laws in Illinois, Michigan, and Kansas, the California constitution made the state board of equalization responsible for assessing all railroad property but left the actual collection of the tax up to local officials.[42] After county officials collected the tax and forwarded the money to the state treasurer, the board of equalization would then redistribute those revenues back to the individual counties in proportion to the mileage of track in each one.[43]

The counties' dependence on the old way of doing things, whereby each county had been free to make its own arrangements with the railroad regarding property tax assessments, became immediately apparent when the railroads refused to pay their taxes under the new constitution. As the state controller put it, "The whole revenue system of the several counties was disarranged thereby; the ordinary obligations of the counties could not be fully met, and in many of the counties the public schools were closed for want of funds."[44] When the railroads refused to pay their taxes in 1880 and 1881, the counties were deprived not only of the revenue to which they had become accustomed but also of the additional money that would have been generated by the new tax on corporate debt instruments and franchises. The state also lost its share of property tax on the assessed value of the railroads.

At first the county tax collectors who had been stiffed by the railroads responded as they would have to any other tax delinquents—by trying to auction off the property in question.[45] The railroads managed to string out their appeals in court for so long, however, that by the time they had been settled, the legal period within which the county assessors could have sold the property for back taxes had elapsed.[46] The following year, 1882, the same thing happened.[47]

In 1882, after the state board of equalization had won a favorable decision in the California State Supreme Court, the various counties sued the railroads for their back taxes of 1880 and 1881. At that point individual counties began to cut their own deals with the railroad, hoping to get some kind of relief from the fiscal pinch. County supervisors in "most of the counties" ordered their district attorneys to "accept sixty per cent of the taxes due."[48] The state controller, on the other hand, refused to accept such compromise payments "because I believed that, as an officer of the State, I had no right to accept less than the whole amount due the State."[49] The situation grew even more complicated when the state attorney general, Edward C. Marshall, suddenly switched sides and began to support the counties' compromise plan. Marshall even brought suit against Contra Costa County, which had followed the state controller's advice and demanded payment of taxes in full, to force it to accept the railroad's compromise tax payment.[50]

Anti-railroad politicians perceived the railroad tax revolt as a struggle over the basic legal status of the corporations involved.[51] Indeed, some of the lawsuits hinged on that exact question. One of the changes in railroad property taxation introduced by the constitution of 1879 was the removal of an exemption previously allowed for debt. Because the railroads had been heavily bonded during their construction, most of their capital was in the form of debt. Under the old California constitution, the railroads had been exempt from paying taxes on that capital because the old constitution allowed the deduction of debts from assessments of taxable property. The new constitution continued that protection for all citizens but expressly revoked it for corporations.[52] Although the state supreme court upheld the distinction in 1882, the railroad appealed to the U.S. Supreme Court. Two of the resulting cases, *San Mateo v. Southern Pacific Railroad Co.*[53] and *Santa Clara County v. Southern Pacific Railroad,* resulted in decisions that assured the privileged status of corporations in American society.[54]

In the *San Mateo* case, the railroad hired former New York senator Roscoe P. Conkling as counsel. Conkling, who had helped write the Fourteenth Amendment to the U.S. Constitution, claimed that the original intent of the amendment's framers had been to afford corporations the same protections as natural persons.[55] According to that argument, the California constitution of 1879 had violated the Fourteenth Amendment by depriving corporations of equal protection under the law in taxing their debts but not the debts of natural persons. In *Santa Clara County v. Southern Pacific Railroad,* which was decided in 1886, the Court declared that the Fourteenth Amendment's equal protection clause extended to corporations as well as natural persons.[56] Thus, the landmark case that determined that American corporations had the same rights as natural persons originated in a lawsuit over state corporation taxes.

The state and the counties felt the fiscal pain of the railroad tax revolt for a decade afterward. The controller repeated the same complaint year after year, about the "heavy deficiency in the receipts to the General Fund, School Fund, and Interest and Sinking Fund, owing to the refusal of the Central and Southern Pacific and other railroad companies to pay the taxes levied upon them by the law."[57] The railroads made various payments over the years—sometimes paying the whole tax levied, sometimes offering a compromise payment, sometimes paying nothing. The entire imbroglio remained unresolved until 1893, when the state legislature reassessed all the unpaid railroad taxes.[58] A U.S. Supreme Court decision of June 1896 affirmed that reassessment and ended the controversy.[59]

The confrontation between California and the Southern Pacific Railroad exemplified the two problems with corporate taxation as it obtained throughout most of the United States in the 1870s: Corporate capital in the form of stocks and bonds escaped taxation, and local assessors valued corporate property utterly unsystematically. Most states still taxed corporation property the same way they taxed individual property, by assessing real estate and, when they could find them, stocks and bonds. In counties close to corporate headquarters, corporate tax assessments were ridiculously low; in counties far away, they were ludicrously high.

By 1880, only a few states in New England and the Middle Atlantic had a good working relationship with business with regard to taxation. In most of the rest of the country, the everyday operation of the most common tax on business encouraged corruption and confrontation rather than compromise. All that would begin to change in the succeeding two decades, however, as the growth of public services slowly but inexorably forced Americans toward corporation tax reform.

TWO

Progress, Bit by Bit

SCHOOL AND INSANE ASYLUM SPENDING,
1880 TO 1900

The railroad tax revolt of the 1880s deprived average Californians of the most significant service offered by local government in nineteenth-century America. "In many of the counties," the controller declared, "the public schools were closed for want of funds."[1] In most states, city and county school systems depended on state government to levy and distribute the statewide taxes that supplied a fat slice of the annual fiscal pie. As the most expensive and pervasive institutions operated by city and county government, public school systems had the most to lose or gain from tax reform in the late nineteenth century.

After education, the second most expensive state program of the late nineteenth century was caring for the insane. Since the 1840s, insane asylums had housed all sorts of people who were unable either to care for themselves or to get along normally with their families or neighbors for a variety of reasons, ranging from conditions we still think of as mental illnesses to developmental disabilities, drug addiction, or old age. By the last two decades of the nineteenth century, many of the first generation of asylums had grown obsolete and overcrowded. Costly patient supervision and even more expensive new construction made such specialized institutions among the highest-priced projects of almost every state.

Although most state governments maintained some sort of insane asylum and contributed at least a little money to their public schools, their financial commitments varied widely. Some states lavished millions of dollars on their schools and asylums; others begrudged even pennies. In high-spending states, expert government officials in education and mental health care played important roles in raising long-term commitments of public funds for their causes. Elsewhere, a Jeffersonian philosophy of minimal government prevailed.

No matter how much states actually spent, most made progress bit by bit in education and mental health care between 1880 and 1900. School and asylum spending grew incrementally, climbing slowly and steadily as the years went by. Current revenues paid all expenses for these two public services. In many respects, the spending patterns of the last two decades of the century were established in the 1850s and 1860s, when the states first undertook to educate all children and care for all indigent insane citizens. Incremental though it was, the growth of spending on schools and insane asylums still weighed heavily on the rickety fiscal infrastructure of the old property tax. That weight—or, in the Jeffersonian republics, its absence—had a significant effect on corporation tax reforms introduced between 1880 and 1907.

Public schools and insane asylums exemplified the two major mechanisms of state finance in the late nineteenth century. Public school money came from special accounts or "funds," hedged about with very specific restrictions on how the money could be spent. Insane asylum money, on the other hand, came from the "general fund," which paid for everything else the state did—that is, everything else that did not have its own special fund. Before the rise of highway spending, public education represented the largest category of special fund expenditures, and insane asylums usually were the largest single expenditure from the general fund. The politics of public school and insane asylum appropriations drove the incremental expansion of state government between 1880 and 1900.

The policy of subsidizing common schools with state money originated in the Northwest Ordinance of 1787, which reserved for educational purposes the proceeds from the sale of one section of each newly surveyed township. Encouraged by the incentive of federal land grants, most western and northern antebellum states underwrote at least part of common school expenses from land sale revenues.[2] The usual procedure was to place those revenues in an "irreducible" fund and redistribute only the income generated by the investment of that fund. For example, the nucleus of the Massachusetts common school fund consisted of proceeds of Maine land sales in 1834, to which had been added various stocks.[3] New York established its common school fund in 1805 with the proceeds of the sale of 500,000 acres of state land.[4] The younger western states started school funds with federal land grants they received upon statehood.[5]

Many northern states began moving toward free public education in the 1850s. In 1851, for example, New York passed a law requiring the state to raise and redistribute among the counties $800,000 annually for school purposes.[6] The following year, California levied a half-mill (five cents per hundred dollars of valuation) property tax for common schools.[7] By the 1860s, both states had abolished tuition fees or "rate bills" altogether in favor of state-supported free school systems.

In 1866, California superintendent of public instruction John Swett led a successful petition campaign to convince the state legislature to raise the state school tax from five cents to eight cents per hundred dollars of assessed valuation. Significantly, the 1866 law also raised the county tax limit from twenty-five to thirty cents her hundred dollars to allow higher school taxes. The combination of higher state and county school taxes allowed common schools to eliminate tuition charges in California, prompting Swett to announce triumphantly that the 1866–67 school year marked "the transition period of California from rate-bill common schools to an American free school system."[8] Likewise, in 1856 New York replaced its $800,000 tax levy with a fixed tax rate of 7.5 cents per hundred dollars, which it raised to 17.5 cents per hundred dollars in 1867.[9] The Empire State also legally abolished rate bills in 1867.[10]

State expenditures for public school purposes grew between 1880 and 1900 largely because of new commitments to free public education that were made in the heat of the 1870s. In 1874, for example, California took the final step in creating its extensive state system of common school funding by setting the annual per pupil state appropriation for common schools at $7, to be raised by taxation over and above any income of the common school fund. That law made California's school tax an "automatic" tax; the rate was determined by the school census and the property valuation, not by the state legislature.[11] In 1875, Wisconsin passed legislation committing the state school fund to underwrite half of the expenses of any free high school established in the state.[12] The same year, New Jersey amended its state constitution, adding the following sentence: "The legislature shall provide for the maintenance and support of a thorough and efficient system of free public schools for the instruction of all the children in this State between the ages of five and eighteen years."[13] By

TABLE 1. Annual Common School Spending from All Sources and Percentage of School Revenues from Local Taxes, Selected States and Years, 1874 to 1900

	1874		1880		1885		1890		1895		1900	
	Total	Local Tax	Total	Local Tax	Total	Local Tax	Total	Local Tax	Total	Local Tax	Total	Local Tax
East												
Massachusetts	$2.74	97%	$2.28	93%	$3.12	96%	$3.39	97%	$4.22	98%	$4.88	97%
New York	$1.80	64%	$1.65	65%	$2.11	72%	$2.68	75%	$3.05	65%	$3.96	69%
New Jersey	$1.62	41%	$1.35	35%	$1.63	37%	$2.12	38%	$2.69	49%	$3.48	61%
Pennsylvania	$1.67	92%	$1.40	n/a	$1.77	n/a	$2.26	76%	$3.25	57%	$3.38	59%
South												
Tennessee	$0.52	n/a	$0.39	n/a	$0.52	58%	$0.79	13%	$0.82	n/a	$0.86	n/a
Alabama	—	n/a	$0.33	31%	$0.33	27%	$0.54	32%	$0.39	18%	$0.50	n/a
Mississippi	$0.78	21%	$0.59	59%	$0.62	58%	$0.79	38%	$0.89	14%	$0.88	37%
Midwest												
Illinois	$2.08	72%	$1.85	52%	$2.59	77%	$2.79	74%	$3.63	86%	$3.05	87%
Michigan	$1.63	58%	$1.38	66%	$2.19	59%	$2.34	73%	$2.67	70%	$2.98	72%
Wisconsin	$1.19	83%	$1.34	67%	$1.89	61%	$2.06	72%	$2.91	74%	$2.62	76%
Great Plains												
North Dakota	—	0%	—	0%	—	0%	$3.15	73%	$4.20	64%	$4.73	64%
South Dakota	—	0%	—	0%	—	0%	$3.35	81%	$4.46	75%	$3.96	78%
Nebraska	$2.53	79%	$1.99	52%	$3.07	67%	$2.93	51%	$3.50	67%	$4.09	62%
Kansas	$1.57	72%	$1.49	49%	$2.41	60%	$3.19	84%	$3.43	88%	$3.11	88%
Far West												
Nevada	$1.80	n/a	$2.88	n/a	$2.55	68%	$3.24	65%	$4.48	43%	$5.25	6%
Oregon	$1.62	66%	$1.43	58%	$2.36	n/a	$2.36	71%	$3.38	71%	$3.82	73%
California	$2.22	63%	$2.69	40%	$3.21	36%	$3.94	46%	$4.48	48%	$4.60	54%

SOURCE: Calculated by the author based on U.S. Department of the Interior, *Report of the Commissioner of Education* (Washington, D.C.: GPO), selected years.
NOTE: Total school spending is shown in real dollars per capita. All figures are for school years ending in the spring of the indicated calendar year. "N/A" indicates that data were not included in the Report of the Commissioner of Education. A dash indicates that the state had not yet entered the Union.

1881, school officials were reading papers at the National Education Association's annual meetings declaring free instruction one of the essential characteristics of American school systems.[14]

In addition to the new state taxes introduced in the 1870s, free public schools also derived a large share of their revenues from local taxes. The exact balance between state funding and local funding varied widely from state to state. States such as Massachusetts, Illinois, and Kansas derived 80–97 percent of their public school revenues from local taxation (Table 1). In most states, the localities footed 60 or 70 percent of the school bill. In other states—including California, New Jersey, Tennessee, Alabama, and Mississippi—the state paid more than half the cost of the public school system.

The balance between state and local funding was not necessarily related to the absolute amount of money spent on schools in a given state. Massachusetts, for example, remained one of the biggest school spenders throughout the late nineteenth century and paid almost its entire school bill with local taxes. California, on the other hand, kept pace with Massachusetts' school spending but funded its schools largely at the state level.

The South was a special case. Unlike the North, the South had never had a tradition of free common schools. Wealthy white children went to private tutors or religious academies. In the antebellum South, "free schools" were strictly charity institutions maintained for children who were too poor to afford a real education.[15] Slaves were kept illiterate by law. Only after the Civil War did free public schools begin to appear in the South. Many of those schools were run cooperatively by freedpeople; others were created by the Freedmen's Bureau or by northern religious agencies, such as the American Missionary Association.[16] Faced with the task of rebuilding an entire society, Reconstruction state governments had few resources to devote to creating school systems from nothing. Towns and counties usually refused to levy taxes required to operate public schools, leaving support of the schools to already-struggling state governments.[17] With the departure of the last federal troops in 1877 and the election of "Redeemer" governments, what little funding public education received in the South virtually dried up. After 1876, for example, Mississippi Democrats shifted primary responsibility for public school funding from the state to localities.[18]

That was the context in which states such as Tennessee, Alabama, and Mississippi spent only a tenth as much on schools as Massachusetts and California. As Table 1 shows, localities contributed only a tiny fraction of that already-minuscule amount. In the late nineteenth century, southern state governments carried the entire financial load of public schools, whereas northern state governments merely supplemented the school revenues of poorer counties. As the U.S. Commissioner of Education remarked in 1893, "what is a merely incidental source of supply in the North is made in the South the chief reliance."[19]

Education was the single largest item of expenditure for most state governments. Even in the South, Mississippi dedicated 40–60 percent of total state expenditures to education. Education took up half of every dollar spent by New Jersey and Kansas in the late nineteenth century. Most other states dedicated one-quarter to one-half of all annual expenditures to keeping their common schools free of charge. States with local systems of school finance—including Tennessee, Massachusetts, Illinois, and Oregon—rarely dedicated more than 10 percent of total state expenditures to education.[20]

Between 1880 and 1900, school spending grew slowly. As the California state controller pointed out in 1877, with his state's "automatic" school tax system, "the tax levy for State school purposes must grow with the increasing number of children."[21] In addition to rising school-age populations, new programs—especially free high schools—drove up school spending. The extent of state support for such institutions varied widely. California's 1879 constitution, for example, authorized free high schools but also specifically restricted the state school fund; it could be used only for the primary grades.[22] More radical attempts to revise the practices of rural schools did not come until the 1910s.

Actual amounts spent by state governments on education ranged from almost four dollars per capita per year in Nevada (clearly a statistical artifact of the state's tiny population) to just a few cents per capita in Tennessee and Illinois. Over time, spending curves for almost every state went up slowly but surely. Only the Dakotas, which were admitted as states in 1889, and southern states deviated from the pattern of incremental growth.[23]

State constitutions usually dictated the distribution of school fund money with very specific formulas that were based on attendance or an annual school census, so school spending bills tended to be less politicized in state legislatures. Although state legislators often wrangled over school-related issues such as textbook selection, mandatory attendance, and required subjects (especially religion), school expenditures at the state level benefited all districts equally because they had to be distributed on the basis of student population.

That was not the case with general fund expenditures such as insane asylums. Unlike common schools, insane asylums could be located only in a few spots around the state, so only certain legislative districts benefited economically from their establishment. As one New York farmer noted in 1893, he and his fellows near Syracuse had thought the new Willard Asylum was "going to be a great benefit to them—they were going to sell all their produce, etc."[24] Any state legislator would have been glad to bring his district an expensive new state institution.

To carry off such a coup, a politician had to get an appropriation from the general fund, from which insane asylum money usually came. Unlike special funds such as the common school fund, the general fund carried no constitutional restrictions on how it might be used. In some states, such as Massachusetts, the general fund was relatively small compared to the special funds; in such states, the general fund accounted for only a fraction of state expenditures, most of which came out of special funds. In other states, general fund expenditures could amount to more than half of the state's annual expenditures. In all states, the amount of money actually subject to legislative appropriations was only a part of total state spending in any given year. Most states spent far more on "automatic" appropriations, such as distribution of the common school fund or repayment of various debts, than on general fund appropriations for programs such as insane asylums, prisons, and regulatory agencies.

Yet the general fund received far more political attention because it was subject to appropriation during each legislative session. Because only the general fund was really under the control of legislators in any given session, state finance officials tended to define general fund expenditures as the "expenses" of state government, lumping special fund expenditures into a separate category. In the late nineteenth century that approach made sense because most states paid their current expenses out of the general fund and used special funds to pay back long-term debt.

The process of making general fund appropriations was chaotic. Private interests and state agencies alike vied for lawmakers' attention. State officials, including insane asylum superintendents, lobbied freely for appropriations for their own projects, and lawmakers commonly passed spending bills for individual institutions. The only gatekeeper assigned to the appropriations process was the state controller, who had to submit to the legislature estimates of the upcoming year's expenses. Controllers based their estimates on the preceding year's expenditures by the various state agencies and sometimes made estimates in consultation with the heads of those agencies.[25] Although the lobbying activities of individual institution managers introduced an element of uncertainty into his estimates, in general the controller still expected to be able to make reasonably accurate predictions.

In most states, insane asylums accounted for the single largest expenditure of the general fund. Insane asylums were important not only in the limited capacity in which we understand mental hospitals today—primarily as delivery vehicles for mental health care—but also as an early and extremely important form of general welfare for all kinds of people whose neighbors, families, or friends thought could only live in institutions.[26] States had been caring for this vaguely defined population of "indigent insane" since the 1840s, when reformers such as Dr. Samuel Gridley Howe and Dorothea Dix first made insanity a significant reform issue.[27] In monetary terms, insane asylums could account for as much as 15 percent of a state's total annual expenditures.

Actual expenditures for insane asylums ranged from almost a dollar per person per year in Nevada in 1895 to nothing at all in Nebraska and South Dakota.[28] Like school expenditures, asylum spending grew slowly over time in most states, with the notable exceptions of Tennessee, North Dakota, and New York. In 1887, Tennessee raised its annual spending on insane asylums to almost a dime per person; the fact that such stingy expenditures looked generous compared to those in Mississippi, Alabama, Kansas, Nebraska, and South Dakota spoke volumes about mental health care in the late-nineteenth-century South and Great Plains.

High expenditures did not always reflect reform. Massachusetts spent relatively little on schools or insane asylums. The Bay State's decentralized system for funding schools and insane asylums made it look like one of the Jeffersonian republics of the South or the Great Plains. In fact, that funding structure was adopted by design rather than chance. An early innovator in state-level care for the insane, Massachusetts deliberately shifted responsibility toward the local level in the 1870s in a well-organized campaign to improve the system—led by some of the very men who had invented the asylum in the first place.

The Massachusetts "lunacy reform" movement exemplified the idealism of the generation that had abolished slavery. The spearhead of the movement was veteran abolitionist Franklin Benjamin Sanborn. Sanborn had begun to establish his anti-authoritarian credentials as a student at Harvard, where he rejected membership in Phi Beta Kappa because he considered the honor society an "unjustifiable intellectual aristocracy."[29] In 1856, just a year after graduating from college, he became secretary of the Massachusetts State Kansas Committee, an association formed for the purpose of collecting money, guns, and supplies to support antislavery New Englanders in their guerrilla war against proslavery Missourians in Kansas. In this capacity he met abolitionist guerrilla chieftain John Brown. Along with mental health reformer Samuel Howe, two abolitionist ministers, and two wealthy capitalists, Sanborn helped support Brown's spectacular failure to incite a slave revolt at Harper's Ferry, Virginia, in the fall of 1859. Sanborn, Howe, and the other four backers became publicly known as the "Secret Six."[30]

After the Civil War, Sanborn co-founded the American Social Science Association in 1865 with such lights as fellow Secret Six conspirator Thomas Wentworth Higginson and abolitionist Wendell Phillips. He also helped found the National Conference on Charities and Corrections.[31] In 1863 the governor of Massachusetts appointed Sanborn secretary of the Massachusetts State Board of Charities—the first state agency of its kind in the nation. Sanborn served as chairman of the board from 1874 to 1876 and as state inspector general of charities from 1879 to 1888.[32] From the 1870s to the end of his life, Sanborn churned out numerous works vindicating the deeds of John Brown, as well as articles and editorials for the Springfield *Republican*—the same paper at which David Wells had gotten his start in the late 1840s. Sanborn epitomized the viewpoint of genteel reformers of the late nineteenth century, who believed that good character was the essential requirement for charity administration.[33]

The 1879 movement for Massachusetts asylum reform was a popular revolt against professional asylum managers.[34] Bay State lunacy reformers demanded public scrutiny for asylum managers, easier releases, and stricter controls on commitments. As chair of the State Board of Charities, Sanborn had begun to campaign against large state insane asylums as early as 1875. In 1877, Sanborn laid out his principles in testimony before a legislative inquiry into cost overruns incurred during the construction of the Worcester and Danvers asylums. Citing fellow abolitionist and mental health reformer Samuel Howe, Sanborn declared that he believed that "the prevailing and increasing size and magnificence of these hospitals was in itself an evil" and "considered these palace hospitals, such as that at Danvers, to be too often prisons, under the form and with the cost of palaces."[35]

Massachusetts lunacy reformers also sensationalized cases of wrongful institutionalization and demanded laws that would complicate commitment and simplify release of inmates. During the legislative session of 1879, while the legislature was deliberating a reorganization of the State Board of Charities and a revision of laws governing asylum commitments, Samuel G. Sewall and

Wendell Phillips addressed a mass meeting at Boston's Tremont Temple on "the treatment, or rather the ill-treatment, of the insane."[36] The speakers recited stories of "malicious incarceration on plea of insanity" and concluded with the adoption of several resolutions, including the demand that the legislature "create a commission or commissioners in lunacy . . . who shall have free access to all asylums and patients, and shall have authority to discharge any patient whenever he thinks the patient's health requires it."[37] The meeting nominated two members of the State Board of Charities, Sanborn and Dr. Nathan Allen, and several other lunacy reformers, including Alzine A. Chevaillier, to present its demands to the legislature.

The legislature bowed to the intense political pressure, partly out of fiscal practicality and partly out of partisan politics.[38] Nathan Allen shrewdly pointed out to the incoming Republican governor that his party, coming back into power after Civil War hero Benjamin Butler's controversial Democratic administration, had an opportunity to "do [itself] much credit and, at the same time, do great good" by stealing the Democrats' traditional retrenchment plank.[39] Ultimately, Massachusetts enacted a law consolidating two previously separate agencies, the Board of Charities and the Board of Health, with additional powers, to constitute a new Board of Health, Lunacy, and Charities.

The new agency responded to reformers' demands for easier releases and more decentralized care. Between 1885 and 1888, Sanborn oversaw an experiment in which "insane persons of the chronic and quiet class" boarded with private families instead of living in state asylums.[40] By 1900, Sanborn was still reporting what he considered good results: Two-thirds of those so removed still lived with their host families, one-tenth had become self-supporting, and the rest had gone back into the asylums.[41]

What the reformers wanted, as Chevaillier wrote in one of her many letters to governor-elect John D. Long in late 1879, was to subject asylum superintendents "to criticism, to action, to supervision"; force them to adopt "scientific and humane measures"; and "lessen their autocratic, irresponsible power."[42] Chevaillier clearly regarded the state as an advocate for inmates against self-interested, power-hungry, self-aggrandizing superintendents. Sanborn's own contemptuous characterization of the superintendents' professional association, the American Association of Medical Superintendents of the Insane, as "that medical trades-union" reflected a similar assessment of asylum superintendents.[43] As one member of the Board of Charities and Lunacy and, later, the Board of Insanity, put it, asylum supervision required "not only good character and reputation but also some special fitness for the position in question—some experience in dealing with charitable institutions as well as experience in dealing with matters of general business."[44] Not, it should be noted, medical expertise, but common business sense and good character. The reformers' plans for a decentralized system of small institutions supervised by men of good character would remain in place in Massachusetts through the turn of the twentieth century.

This arrangement was the polar opposite of the state care system that eventually obtained there and in New York. New York's asylum reform campaign of the 1890s illustrated the transition from the nineteenth-century methods of romantic reformers such as Howe and Sanborn to the twentieth-century ascendance of professional experts. Where Massachusetts' reforms of the 1870s had devolved authority to the local level, New York's reforms of the 1890s centralized power at the state level. Where Massachusetts' reforms had reduced spending at the state level, New York's proved extremely expensive. By 1897, New York led the nation in asylum spending, devoting eighty cents to that program for every man, woman, and child in the state. A later legislative commission called New York's asylum reform "the greatest single change" in a "an extraordinary period in the development of the State government," the years from 1880 to 1900.[45] New York's expenditures for care of the insane after 1890 were nonincremental—that is, spending took a sudden leap upward, instead of building bit by bit. The state's insane asylum policy differed from contemporaneous school spending, which rose incrementally. The political campaign for asylum reform in New York revealed the institutional and partisan conditions under which states could undertake nonincremental spending increases.

New York's state mental health care system originated with the construction of a state asylum at Utica in 1843. In 1865, the Empire State expanded its mental health care system by building another state insane asylum and prohibiting all but the state's most urban counties from building or operating their own asylums.[46] The new asylum soon filled up, however, and instead of building another one, in 1871 the legislature rescinded its ban on county asylums, allowing all counties to care for their own chronic insane citizens with the permission of the State Board of Charities.[47]

From 1871 to 1890, New York adopted by default the same decentralized system that Massachusetts used by design. Unlike Massachusetts, however, New York spent little effort in overseeing the quality of care at local institutions. Most mental patients in New York went to Kings, Monroe, or New York County asylums or to poorhouses. A smaller proportion went to the state asylums, and a few went to private asylums. New York, Kings, and Monroe County asylums, which had been exempted from the 1865 law because of the quality of their facilities, housed more than half of the state's insane population by 1889. In that year, the state asylums held about 5,400 patients; the asylums of the three exempt counties had nearly 7,000 inmates, and scattered city and county poorhouses across the state cared for an estimated 3,000 more. Private asylums held 500 residents.[48]

In 1875 the New York State Charities Aid Association (NYSCAA), a private reform society, began calling for the exact opposite of the policy advocated by its Massachusetts counterparts. The NYSCAA drew public attention to the abominable conditions in the county poorhouses and demanded a return to the policy of state care established in 1865.[49] Its efforts, however, met with little success for the next decade. In 1887, Louisa Lee Schuyler, secretary of the association's committee on the insane, revived the campaign. Schuyler and the NYSCAA exemplified the female side of the genteel social reform tradition that Franklin Sanborn represented in Massachusetts. Schuyler had made a public reputation for herself during the Civil War by serving with the U.S. Sanitary Commission, a pioneering medical agency devoted to nursing Union soldiers back to health. After the war, she had continued to pursue public health reform with the mostly female NYSCAA. She modeled her career on that of her friend, famous British nursing pioneer Florence Nightingale.[50]

Schuyler's 1887 report on conditions in county asylums resulted in the introduction of a state care bill in the 1888 session of the state legislature but could not secure the bill's passage.[51] The following year another bill was introduced, but it too failed. Only in 1890, with the publication of the first annual report of the new Commission in Lunacy and its "graphic exposure of the abuses of the county system," did a new state care bill pass the legislature.[52]

The commissioners found incompetent doctors, casual brutality, and routine chaos. One asylum manager defended his mental health care credentials by boasting, "I can walk up to any of our men, however violent they may be, and throw them on their backs, without striking or hurting them. After this treatment, three times out of four they are humbled. If they are not, I let them regain their feet and throw them again, and if this does not answer they are confined to a room."[53] The commissioners also found in the county poorhouses inmates who received no medical attention at all, as well as inmates who were left locked up overnight without access to toilets, "put to bed and left to lie in their filth and excrement until morning."[54]

The *New York Times* attributed the State Care Act's success in 1890 largely

to the lunacy commissioners' report. Significantly, the *Times* added, "It is grat-
ifying that the support of the State Care bill in both branches of the Legislature was non-partisan."[55]

The new law, like the law of 1865, again barred counties from caring for
their own insane populations—with the exception of Kings, New York, and
Monroe counties, which would still retain the option of turning over their insane to the state as well.[56] As the Commissioners in Lunacy wrote in their second report, the law "puts the State's policy relative to its insane citizens back
again upon the same high plane where it was intended to be placed by the passage of the Willard Asylum Act in 1865."[57]

The bill's passage in 1890 did not necessarily guarantee state care for the
insane. Nothing could be done without money, and the necessary appropriations did not come before the legislature until 1891, with the recommendations of the Commission in Lunacy. Before the legislature of 1891 even met,
supervisors of several upstate counties protested the new annual payments they
would have to make to support the patients they sent to the state institution.
"We have as good medical attendance as any State hospital," the Chautauqua
County Board of Supervisors announced defiantly; "our patients have all the
freedom that is consistent with any degree of restraint, and are in as good physical condition as are the inmates of the State hospitals."[58] Upstate counties re-
sisted the State Care Act because they were convinced that they could care for
the insane more cheaply than the state could. Chautauqua County spent only
$1.50 per capita per week to keep inmates in its poorhouse; the State Care Act
specified that counties would pay $4.25 per capita per week for the first three
years of state care.[59] Such parsimoniousness, replied the commissioners, was
false economy. As an example of the inadequacy of county care, they cited
the Chenango County poorhouse, which had burned down shortly after the
passage of the State Care Act as a result of an unsupervised "idiot ward" in-
mate smoking her pipe in bed. The evacuation was sheer chaos, as "the idiots
babbling and jabbering ran down the keepers, who cried the alarm as they
went. . . . The majority of the violent ones, however, made directly for the woods
and for hours afterwards they could be heard screaming and yelling in the adjacent forest." Several died in the fire.[60]

The 1891 appropriation passed. A much larger appropriation was approved in 1893, when county payments ended and the state took over the entire cost of caring for its insane inhabitants. To meet that cost, estimated at
$1.4 million, the state levied a special one-third mill property tax the same
year.[61] Officials in Kings and New York counties, faced with paying a tax for

the support of mental patients from all over the state in addition to paying to support their own insane residents, began to make plans to get out of the insane asylum business and turn over their facilities and their inmates to state control.[62] In 1896 the transfer was complete, and the state became the sole custodian of 15,000 people without the mental wherewithal to take care of themselves. "The practical extension of the State Care Act to all the counties of the State, including Kings and New York," the state controller observed, "marks a new era in the fiscal history of the State."[63]

Thus, New York's unique progressiveness in the area of mental health resulted from a combination of private reform efforts, nonpartisan politics, and the lobbying efforts of state doctors who had a clear professional interest in mental health reform. Schuyler and other private reformers could not have done it alone; after all, they had been campaigning unsuccessfully since 1875. But yoked to the expert authority of the Commission in Lunacy, the nonpartisan strategy of the NYSCAA resulted in a significant nonincremental spending increase. As Schuyler reminded New York mayor Josiah Strong during negotiations for the transfer of the New York City hospital to the state, "For twenty years they [the legislators] have passed every law we have asked for, sooner or later, always as philanthropic measures, never as party measures."[64] For nonincremental expansion such as New York's 1891 State Care Act, nonpartisanship and expert advice would prove crucial factors in other states as well after the dawn of the twentieth century.

Between 1880 and 1900, incremental expenditures for schools and asylums carried out policy initiatives undertaken earlier in the nineteenth century. States that had committed themselves to free public schools in the 1870s paid the costs of rising enrollment. States that had built insane asylums as early as the 1840s continued to support those institutions or, like New York, built new ones and expanded the scope of their services. The costs of fulfilling their promises to educate all children or care for all of the indigent insane gave some state officials additional incentive to revamp their faltering property tax systems. Many of them turned to one form or another of the corporation tax. Other states, in contrast, spent almost nothing on schools or insane asylums— and made little or no effort to get rid of their old property tax systems either. Causal links between specific spending measures and particular varieties of the corporation tax depended on various combinations of spending policies and tax reform campaigns, but a few common factors come to light on closer examination of the revenue experiments that paid for progress, bit by bit.

From Charter-Mongering to Catching Corporate Freeloaders

CORPORATION TAXES, 1880 TO 1907

For old-school tax reformers such as David Wells, the years from 1880 to 1907 were one long nightmare. All he had asked for in 1871 was a rational system for taxation of stocks and bonds—preferably a system that offered generous breaks for his friends in business. What he got instead was an age of economic radicalism of various stripes, from Henry George's single-tax movement to Populist plans for deliberate inflation. Actual tax policies in the various states and localities swung wildly from the business-friendly tax environments of the 1880s to the urban utility crackdowns of the 1900s. Although Wells died in 1898, on the eve of the period's most profound changes, he did live to see several significant departures from the property tax he hated so much.

Not only did state tax systems change between 1880 and 1907, they also began to diverge more and more from each other. Three factors set the corporate states and the Jeffersonian republics on different paths. First, states that spent a lot on schools and insane asylums already were beginning to strain the capacities of the old property tax system. Second, urban states began to require additional income for municipal improvements. Third, in the 1900s northeastern states began to retaliate against corporations for taking advantage of tax breaks granted in the 1880s, while corporate politics in southern and Great

Plains states focused on regulation rather than taxation. By 1907, two distinct styles of business taxation had emerged.

In the 1880s, the nation's growing industrial economy made regional differences increasingly important. The rise of the transcontinental railroad and new technologies in manufacturing intensified regional specialization. Manufacturing dominated the Northeast. The Midwest and Far West had mixed economies centered around the metropolises of Chicago and San Francisco, respectively. The Great Plains and the South were largely agricultural.[1] Depending on the regional economy, each state had different interests with regard to business taxation.

The 1880s brought some relief from the Great Depression of the 1870s, but in the Midwest, Great Plains, and South the same basic tension between the railroads on one hand and farmers and shippers on the other persisted. "In this age," remarked the governor of Kansas in 1887, "railroads make and unmake cities and towns, and hence a flourishing community, on whose commerce and industries the prosperity of hundreds or thousands of people depend, may be destroyed by the building of one or two railways."[2] Local governments in Kansas responded by issuing town and county bonds to aid in the construction of local railroads. The boom times of the early 1880s also tempted individual Kansans to borrow against their property—so much so that by 1890 more than half of all land in the state was mortgaged.[3]

While Kansans responded enthusiastically to railroads in the 1880s, their neighbors were not as friendly. In 1883, for example, the Dakota Territory enacted a gross receipts tax on railroads, but it was declared unconstitutional in 1891, and the new state of North Dakota replaced it with a special tax on railroad property.[4] Midwestern Grangers let the railroads know they were still active in 1885, when an Illinois legislative commission recommended a tax on the gross receipts of utilities, but the legislature failed to adopt it.[5]

In contrast, the industrial states of the Northeast courted the corporations in the 1880s. New York, for example, adopted a capital-stock tax modeled on Pennsylvania's law but formulated to provide maximum incentive for investors to locate in the Empire State. New York legislators initially tried to imitate the Pennsylvania system, "where the entire State revenue is raised by a tax on corporations, copartnerships, etc.—relieving them from local assessment, and at the same time relieving the localities from all taxation for State purposes."[6] City officials preferred, however, to keep the revenues contributed to municipal coffers by old-fashioned general property taxes on corporate land, buildings, and equipment.[7] Compared to the huge bite that the proposed law would take out of local tax bases by making corporate property exempt from local property taxes, the amount of state tax the new reform proposed to relieve was minuscule. Legislators finally agreed on a corporation tax but set the rate too low to support the entire cost of state government. They also retained local officials' authority to tax corporate property.[8] New York's great compromise of 1880 was at least a partial victory for urban legislators because they got to keep their big tax bases of corporate real estate. Like the Massachusetts and Pennsylvania corporate tax laws, it also benefited capitalists because stocks of domestic companies were no longer taxable in the hands of investors.

New York legislators also had taken every precaution to get business on their side. According to the state comptroller, "The provisions of the act, including the rate of tax, were intentionally made favorable to the corporations."[9] The rate, in fact, ranged from 7.5 to 15 cents per hundred dollars of capital stock (par value), whereas the general property tax rate was about 25 cents per hundred dollars of valuation.[10] In addition to its low rate, the new tax law also exempted manufacturing and mining companies to attract them to build plants in the Empire State.

New York's manufacturing exemption set the tone for the Middle Atlantic states' tax measures of the 1880s. Most of those laws aimed to attract investment and encourage economic growth. New York's business-friendly exemption of manufacturing companies itself merely imitated Pennsylvania's 1879 exemption for limited partnerships engaged in manufacturing. In 1885, Pennsylvania even expanded that exemption to include all corporations engaged in manufacturing.[11] In the 1880s, corporation tax policy in the Northeast was essentially a race to the bottom among states trying to prevent capital flight from within their own borders and simultaneously attract investment away from their neighbors.

The most infamous example of such a competitive state tax policy was New Jersey's incorporation law of 1883. To attract large corporations, the law imposed an extremely low fee (two cents per hundred dollars of valuation) on companies seeking to incorporate in the Garden State.[12] It was a high-volume, low-price approach to maximizing corporation tax revenues. New Jersey's "charter-mongering" strategy worked so well that it funded a large share of the state's expenses and may have contributed to the great merger wave of the 1890s.[13]

Just a year after New Jersey opened its doors to the nation's corporations, it negotiated a railroad tax deal that showed all the hallmarks of a classic corporation tax. The railroad tax of 1884 made a compromise between the state, localities, and business. The tax took the job of assessing railroad property away from the localities and centralized it at the state level. It classified railroad property into several categories and taxed them at a single rate: fifty cents per hundred dollars of valuation. It divided the revenue between the state and the cities through which the railroad passed. The state got more reliable tax revenue from railroad property, the railroads got lower tax rates and assessments, and localities got a piece of the revenue.[14]

In the 1890s, new departures in corporation tax policy further distinguished corporate states from Jeffersonian republics. In the corporate states of the Northeast and Midwest, the growth of municipal utility projects prompted many cities to seek new sources of revenue by revising their tax laws. Their attempts to do so frequently resulted in public scandals over the ways in which corporations had taken advantage of tax breaks created in the 1880s or before. In contrast, the Jeffersonian republics of the Great Plains and South, which lacked big cities and high state spending on education or mental health care, focused more on railroad regulation than new sources of revenue. The legal status of corporations was a critical issue in Progressive politics in all sections of the nation, but only in the Northeast and Midwest—where high state spending on schools and asylums combined with expensive municipal projects—did the struggle focus on taxation.

Comparison of corporation tax reform among three states—Wisconsin, New Jersey, and Kansas—illustrates the importance of municipal improvements on one hand and corporate tax-dodging on the other in guiding state tax policy before 1907. Corporate tax-dodging was the key issue on which the Progressive movements in the former two states were founded. In contrast, the Progressive movement in Kansas was more concerned with regulating corporations than taxing them. The details of tax reform in these three states between 1895 and 1907 highlight the importance of municipal expenditures and the specific political problems of corporations in each state.

The Panic of 1893 hit Wisconsin as hard as it did the rest of the country. The depression brought together several disparate reform groups under the umbrella of property tax reform. In 1895, the Wisconsin state legislature made the property tax situation even worse by placing taxation of street railways on the same basis as that on steam railroads. The state took over assessment of street railway property and taxed it at a single rate, based on gross receipts; in exchange, corporations were exempt from local taxation. Localities got most of the resulting revenue, which did not amount to much.[15] The practical effect of the law was to exempt street railways from local taxation because the new state rate of taxation was so much lower than the old local rates. In fact, the chief advocate of the new tax was Henry C. Payne, president of the Milwaukee Street Railway.

Payne's goal was to escape the city's ever-increasing property taxes. Milwaukee, like other American cities in the 1880s and 1890s, had issued large bonds to underwrite street paving, street lighting, and sewer projects. To pay off the debt, the city had to impose high property taxes. As some of the city's largest property owners, utility and street railway companies bore a heavy share of the tax load. The removal of their property from the city's overall tax base drove up everyone else's property taxes. That was the very development that reformers had been working so hard to stop for the preceding two years. Payne's opponents united as the Milwaukee Municipal League.[16] This reform movement became the nucleus of the Wisconsin Progressive Party. In 1900, its candidate, Robert M. "Battlin' Bob" La Follette, was elected governor. A national leader in the Progressive movement, La Follette later became a U.S. senator and candidate for the Progressive Party's presidential nomination.

After their statewide victory in 1900, Wisconsin Progressives proceeded with their campaign against corporate tax dodgers. In 1903, after a lengthy legislative battle with the railroads, Wisconsin changed the basis of steam railroad tax assessments from gross receipts to property values, significantly increasing receipts from that source.[17] In 1905, at La Follette's urging, the legislature reversed the previous decade's street railway act by putting street railways and electric companies on the *ad valorem* basis of assessment—taxing them on property value instead of income and effectively raising their taxes.[18]

Wisconsin Progressives were not alone in thinking the compromise of corporation taxation was looking more and more like a free ride for big business. As cities such as Milwaukee undertook expensive improvements, urban progress drove up property taxes. Yet while individual taxpayers winced at their rising bills, utilities kept on smiling. Thanks to the compromise of the state corporation tax, utilities remained exempt from rising local property taxes. Over the years, the inequality between the taxes paid by corporations and those paid by everyone else grew.

In 1906, New Jersey faced a situation that was very similar to that in Wisconsin. The same pattern of corporate freeloading under cover of the state corporation tax developed in Jersey City that had appeared in Milwaukee, although this time it involved steam railroads instead of street railways. In New Jersey, as in Wisconsin, corporate abuse of the state corporation tax to avoid rising local tax rates provoked a dramatic political response, giving rise to a state Progressive movement whose momentum eventually helped bring Woodrow Wilson to national prominence.[19]

Since 1884 New Jersey railroads had paid the nominal state tax rate of 1.5 percent, with proceeds divided between the state and localities through which the railroad passed. As a result, municipalities along the way lost a valuable tax base in the form of railroad property. In 1904, Jersey City mayor Mark M. Fagan, a former assistant undertaker who had risen through the ranks of the Republican machine, began to lobby state legislators for railroad tax reform. Fagan helped found the New Jersey Mayors' Equal Taxation League and created a faction in the Republican Party known as the "New Idea." In 1906, thanks to the pressure of New Idea politicians, the legislature passed the Perkins Act, which raised the rate to the average rate of local taxation in the state and nearly tripled the state's railroad tax revenues in a single year.[20] Like Wisconsin's 1905 street railway revaluation measure, New Jersey's Perkins Act turned the tables on an existing corporation tax that corporations previously had used to avoid rising local taxes. Unlike the corporate tax revision of Wisconsin, however, the New Jersey law of 1906 directed any revenue generated by the tax reform into the state public school fund, not to the municipalities involved. Thus, in New Jersey a measure that began as a campaign of urban Progressivism ended up funding state-level public services.

Ingenious political maneuvering around the passage of the New Jersey law reminded everyone involved of the flaws of the old property tax. New Jersey's first railroad tax reform act was passed in 1905. Opponents of tax reform simultaneously passed a companion law, however, placing a ceiling of 1.5 percent on local property tax rates.[21] On paper, the tax rate ceiling negated the railroad tax measure by restricting the statewide rate of taxation to what the railroads had been paying before. The stratagem failed, however, because of a well-known structural weakness of the property tax: inaccurate assessments.

Two numbers determined the actual amount a person paid on his or her property taxes: the rate and the assessment. The rate was set by the legislature, but the assessment was determined by local tax assessors. A rate ceiling would be effective only if assessments were consistent. The problem was that assessments never were. Tax officials had complained about that since before David Wells published his report in 1871. Because assessors were locally elected officials, they usually assessed property at a mere fraction of its true value to stay popular and get reelected.

Faced with a rate ceiling of 1.5 percent, however, local tax officials in New

Jersey simply raised the assessments until they derived sufficient revenue to meet the year's municipal expenditures. As one New Jersey board of trade bluntly put it in a published pamphlet, "There must be as many hundred dollars of assessed valuations as $1.50 will go into the total amount of the budget."[22] With the rate capped, assessments skyrocketed. Widespread public outrage at the skyrocketing property assessments of 1905 became an important factor in the law's revocation in 1906 and simultaneous passage of the more effective Perkins Act.

Unlike Wisconsin's 1905 street railway revaluation act, New Jersey's 1906 Perkins Act did not bring more revenue directly to municipalities. Whereas Wisconsin revised its corporation tax to benefit localities, New Jersey directed extra revenues derived from its railroad revaluation act to benefit the state public school fund.[23]

When Wisconsin's neighbor Michigan raised its railroad tax rate in 1901, almost doubling its revenues from that source, the state constitution required all corporation tax receipts to benefit the public school fund, so the Great Lakes State's tax reform had the same effect as New Jersey's.[24] When Michigan and New Jersey revised their corporation tax laws to catch corporate freeloaders, they used the proceeds to pay for educational programs undertaken in the last two decades of the nineteenth century. The railroad tax reforms of New Jersey and Michigan paid the price of progress statewide, while Wisconsin's went to subsidize municipal improvements.

Things were much different in Kansas. The depression of 1893 had a much more radical political effect on the farms of the Great Plains than it had in the cities of the Midwest. First, the Great Plains already had a highly competitive third-party movement, in the form of Populism, even before 1893. The Populist agenda demanded outright government ownership of utilities such as railroads. Kansas had established a maximum railroad freight law in the 1860s and a railroad commission in 1883. In 1897, a Populist state legislature lost patience with the railroad commission and created a new agency, the Court of Visitation. The court had the power to establish rates, classify freight, and bar railroads from making "unnecessary improvements." Although the Court of Visitation was ruled unconstitutional by the U.S. Supreme Court in 1900,[25] the fact that such a law had passed in the first place illustrated the depth of feeling against railroads in Kansas.

Railroad regulation continued to be an issue in the first decade of the twentieth century. In 1904, a reform faction of Republicans known as the Kansas Republican League succeeded in electing Edward W. Hoch governor. Hoch advocated property tax reform and railroad regulation, but he achieved only the latter goal during his first term. He was reelected in 1906 with the support of the Kansas Federation of Commercial Interests (a group of Wichita shippers), the Kansas Civic League, and the Square Deal Club, all of which were interested in railroad reform. In 1907, the legislature created a state tax commission, mainly because the Square Dealers wanted it to reassess railroad property.[26]

What Kansas Progressives really wanted was railroad regulation. They got that with the 1905 law that strengthened the powers of the railroad commission. Tax reform was almost a second thought. In fact, the immediate result of the new tax commission was an across-the-board hike in all property assessments, resulting in higher taxes not only for the railroads but for all property owners. The new assessments were almost six times higher than those for the previous year.[27] In 1908, when this unintended consequence of the tax commission law became evident, Hoch hastily called a special session of the state legislature to limit the new assessments to levels that would produce a total revenue not to exceed 102 percent of the amount collected the preceding year.[28]

For corporations, the Kansas tax commission law meant few changes. The new assessments generally evened out because the commissioners found that some corporations had been assessed too much in the past and others too little. In general, the decisions of the Kansas tax commission followed standards similar to those used by states such as Massachusetts and New York that had more elaborate tax laws. In assessing a corporation, the tax commission took into account "material and supplies on hand, rolling-stock, moneys, credits, and all other property of the companies . . . reported cost of construction, gross and net earnings, operating and maintenance expenses."[29] That procedure was very similar to the function of the Massachusetts corporation law, even down to the terminology of "excess value" as determined by corporate income. Yet even though the Kansas tax commission exercised significant discretion in applying the property tax to corporations, its establishment did not create any new taxes directed specifically at corporate property.

The main difference between the Kansas tax commission law and the corporation tax laws of Wisconsin and New Jersey was that in the latter states, corporation tax laws generated new revenues for municipal improvements (in Wisconsin) and the state school fund (in New Jersey). In contrast, the tax commission law of Kansas did not single out corporations as a source of new revenue; instead, it increased assessments across the board. In Wisconsin and New

Jersey, corporations generated political opposition by taking egregious advantage of tax breaks created for them earlier in the nineteenth century. In Kansas, the railroads provoked Progressives by their rate-setting policies rather than their efforts to escape taxation.

Wisconsin and New Jersey adopted tax strategies that were characteristic of corporate states. They imposed new taxes specifically on corporations that were designed to fund new programs. In Wisconsin, the new taxes allocated revenues to city coffers to help pay for street lighting, paving, and sewer systems. In New Jersey, those taxes went to pay for public schools. Kansas, in contrast, took a Jeffersonian approach. Instead of tapping new corporate sources of revenue with innovative taxes, the Sunflower State merely renovated its existing methods of collecting taxes on all types of property.

In the South, conditions similar to those in Kansas obtained. Southern Progressivism focused on regulation rather than taxation. The dramatic anticorporation campaigns of Alabama governor Braxton B. Comer and Mississippi governor James K. Vardaman had more to do with railroad freight rates than with corporation tax-dodging.[30] Nor had those states initiated any significant new spending programs on services such as public education or mental health care during the 1880s or 1890s, so they had no fiscal incentive to impose new corporation taxes during the same period.

The states of the Far West, like those of the Northeast and the Midwest, did engage in significant public-service spending in the 1880s and 1890s. Although they did not undertake corporation tax revisions on the same scale as the northeastern and midwestern states, Oregon and California did begin to move toward corporation taxes after 1900. In 1903, for example, Oregon imposed a fee on the organization of corporations similar to those charged by New Jersey and New York. Unlike the infamous New Jersey measure of 1883, however, the Oregon law was enacted mainly as a revenue measure.[31] In 1905, California followed suit with a similar revenue-driven corporation license tax.[32]

One more example from the industrial Northeast completes the picture of corporation taxes in the years before 1907. According to state tax laws as of January 1899, New York public service corporations had it tough. Street railways, telegraph companies, and pipelines paid local property taxes on their real estate, buildings, and equipment. Street railways also paid an additional "franchise tax" of 1 percent on gross earnings and an additional 3 percent on dividends declared over 4 percent.[33] Although those provisions looked good on paper, in practice New York street railways were getting almost as much of a free ride as their Wisconsin counterparts in those days.

The compromise of New York's corporation tax reserved taxation of corporate capital to the state. Corporate capital, where the real value of the nation's new industrial enterprises was accumulating, therefore was exempt from local taxation, and corporations paid only the nominal rate of fifteen cents per hundred dollars of valuation. By contrast, the average rate of local taxation on property was about two and a half dollars per hundred dollars of valuation, or 167 times higher.[34] Thus, despite their 1 percent gross earnings taxes, street railways and other urban utilities still paid a ridiculously low rate of taxation on their corporate capital.

In 1899, Republican governor Theodore Roosevelt began to detect a case of corporate tax-dodging. State senator John Ford of New York City had proposed a bill in the legislature to define the right to lay pipes and rails in public streets as a "special franchise," taxable with other forms of property. In light of other corporation bills before the legislature, including New York City mass transit and the monopolistic Astoria Gas corporate franchise, Roosevelt decided to support the Ford bill. The "special franchise tax" would be assessed by the state, but the revenue would go to municipalities. The special franchise tax would replace the unproductive capital-stock tax on transportation and transmission companies. Like Wisconsin's 1905 law that switched street railway valuations to the *ad valorem* system, New York's 1899 special franchise act increased the urban tax base dramatically. "No enactment of modern times," gushed the state tax commissioners in 1901, "is more popular with the people of this state."[35] Or, they might have added, more unpopular with transit corporations—although manufacturers supported it.[36] The Brooklyn *Eagle* prophesied that the law would "make New York State quotable with Kansas, Nebraska and Missouri in the scale of communistic and social legislation, as a state for capital to shun, for investments to abandon and for enterprise and confidence to desert."[37]

In addition to the special franchise tax of 1899, in 1901 New York renegotiated corporation taxes on out-of-state or "foreign" companies, trust companies, and banks. The new tax on those financial corporations served three functions. First, it provided a new source of revenue for the cash-strapped state. Second, it discouraged foreign companies from coming into the state and encouraged them to incorporate in New York instead. Third, it relieved banks from local taxation on their deposits, which previously had been assessed at 10–110 percent of face value by the localities.[38] The tax was phenomenally successful in all three respects.[39]

Unlike the special franchise tax of 1899, which addressed the needs of municipal progress, the new taxes of 1901 addressed the needs of state progress. When New York assumed responsibility for the care of its entire population of homeless lunatics in the 1890s, it incurred a massive new expense that did not fit the traditional model of incremental spending growth. The special legislative commission that recommended the new taxes in 1900 clearly explained that the state's growing expenditures prompted the new taxes. In addition to the state's current receipts, the commissioners noted, "the State will require about three millions of dollars. To provide for this, we propose to levy a tax of one per cent upon the stock of national banks, State banks and trust companies."[40] Trusts, banks, and foreign corporations paid the price of New York's progress in caring for its mentally ill citizens in the 1890s and 1900s.

The share of state revenues derived from corporation taxes clearly distinguished corporate states from Jeffersonian republics. From 1880 to 1909, the corporation tax supplied 25–60 percent of annual state revenues in Pennsylvania, Massachusetts, Wisconsin, and Michigan.[41] Pennsylvania and Massachusetts had pioneered the corporation tax earlier in the nineteenth century and made few revisions. The share of Pennsylvania's revenue contributed by the corporation tax grew incrementally, more or less as the Keystone State's school and insane asylum spending did. In Massachusetts that share declined—not as a result of falling revenues but because other forms of receipts, mainly bond sales, shot up around 1894. Wisconsin and Michigan, also old veterans of corporate taxation in the form of their longstanding railroad taxes, showed the same relatively large and stable contribution to state receipts from the corporations. The jump in the proportion of New York's annual receipts from corporation taxes between 1900 and 1904 reflected new revenues from the tax on financial corporations imposed to pay for the state's insane asylum program.

In the Jeffersonian republics of the South, Great Plains, and Far West, corporation taxes contributed a negligible share to state receipts. Of those states, only Tennessee and California consistently collected more than 10 percent of their state receipts from corporations. Illinois, Nebraska, and South Dakota received nothing from corporation taxes during the entire period.

Between 1880 and 1907, the function of state corporation taxes shifted from attracting investment to supporting progress, in the form of new public services offered at the municipal or state level. Although most corporation taxes of the 1880s improved a state's business climate, popular hostility against corporate tax-dodgers after 1900 prompted many states to renegotiate the compromise of the corporation tax. Railroads and urban utilities in particular had taken advantage of the low rate and exemption from local property taxation offered by the state corporation tax. They became the major targets of corporation tax reform in the first decade of the twentieth century. Proceeds from higher taxes levied on those enterprises paid for municipal water and sewer systems, streetlights, and paved streets. They also underwrote state public school funds and New York's new system of state insane asylums.

The years from 1880 to 1907 witnessed the subtle beginnings of a change in the relationship between business and government. Around the turn of the twentieth century, Americans began to realize that business corrupted politics.[42] In the late nineteenth century, legislative lobbying often had shaded into bribery, especially in debates over laws that could affect significant business interests. Progressive campaigns for corporation tax reform in Wisconsin, New York, and New Jersey condemned behind-the-scenes influence on the part of business lobbyists in state legislatures. Traditional forms of corporate influence on state government came under increasing fire.

Corporate taxation was one of the factors that led to the creation of a new form of corporate influence on government. The new style of corporate influence was less confrontational and more cooperative. Instead of relying on bribery or threats applied to individual legislators, the new corporate influence involved voluntary associations and independent experts who offered advice to the administrative agencies that proliferated at every level of government. In the first decade of the twentieth century, the most significant such association that formed to bring business guidance to government tax policy was the National Tax Association (NTA).

In 1907, at its first national conference in Columbus, Ohio, the NTA brought together businessmen and government officials to discuss the best practices and theories of taxation and to advise state agencies and legislatures of their findings. Members of two existing organizations, the New York Tax Reform Association (NYTRA) and the Ohio Chamber of Commerce, supplied most of the delegates to the first meeting of the NTA. The NYTRA provided office space for the NTA. One of the leaders of the NYTRA was Edwin R. A. Seligman, who had advised Theodore Roosevelt and the legislature on New York's 1899 special franchise tax and who later became president of the NTA.[43] The annual meetings of the NTA became an important clearinghouse for the latest ideas about taxation from professional economists, longtime public servants, and powerful businessmen. During the succeeding two decades, the NTA exercised significant influence over the theory and practice of corporate taxation.

By the time of the NTA's first meeting, an important trend in state expenditures already was developing that would fundamentally reshape the public services of the American state. Costlier than schools, more expensive than insane asylums, public demand for the almighty paved road was still a distant rumble on the fiscal horizon in 1907. Before long, however, it would become a deafening roar.

FOUR

The Second Era of Internal Improvements

TRANSPORTATION SPENDING, 1890 TO 1929

In the 1890s, while public schools and state insane asylums slowly expanded, a handful of bicycle enthusiasts began a political movement that would grow into the most expensive public service the American states had ever seen. Along the way, these "wheelmen" were joined by the automobile industry, highway engineers, and a growing army of motorists who were sick of getting stuck in the mud. Highway advocates would find the new political tools of direct democracy, the initiative and the referendum, extremely useful in raising public expenditures for transportation. With those levers, they would overturn a half-century of pay-as-you-go financing and government disengagement from major transportation projects in almost every state. By the onset of the Great Depression, state governments would be racking up enormous debts in the name of what novelist Sinclair Lewis called the Great God Motor.[1]

Differences in state transportation systems highlighted the divergence of the corporate states from the Jeffersonian republics. The main differences were timing and magnitude. Corporate states devoted far more resources to the project much earlier than did their Jeffersonian counterparts. In corporate states, transportation advocates built powerful electoral coalitions and took advantage of the initiative and the referendum to bring their states earlier and larger infrastructure projects. In Jeffersonian republics, the lure of matching federal funds appealed to the traditional parsimony of the state governments, encouraging them to invest in highways only after the first World War.

The details of transportation development in the corporate states illustrate how interest groups used the institutional mechanism of the initiative and the referendum to initiate early state-level investments in transportation. Although the Good Roads movement was nationwide in the early 1890s, at first it succeeded only in the most urban states, such as Massachusetts and New Jersey. In corporate states with stronger agricultural contingents in their legislatures, such as New York and Wisconsin, it got off to a much slower start. In 1892, New Jersey became the first state to create a system for providing financial aid to assist counties with road construction.[2] The New Jersey law exemplified state road acts of the 1890s. Counties initiated improvements and made construction contracts, and the state provided engineering expertise and oversight. Owners of property next to the improvement paid a tenth of the cost, the state paid a third, and the county paid the rest.[3] Massachusetts followed suit a year later. As in New Jersey, the Massachusetts State Highway Commission followed methods advocated by Good Roads enthusiasts nationwide.[4] Towns desiring state assistance in paving their roads applied to the highway commission, which sent the state engineer out to examine the surveys and plans. After approving the plans and estimating the cost, the state commission then contracted with the town or helped to arrange a contract between the town and a private subcontractor to do the actual work.[5] The state and the town then split the cost: The state paid 75 percent and the town paid the rest.[6] By the end of the commission's first year of operation, it had started work on thirty-seven separate road projects, each about a mile long.[7]

Good Roads advocates campaigned in New York as well in the early 1890s, but anti-road feelings among the Empire State's farmers prevented enactment of a state-aid law until 1898, despite the coaxing of several successive governors from both parties. In 1890, for example, governor David B. Hill proposed that the state construct an extensive network of state-owned roads that would connect every county seat, but the bill sank without a trace in the legislature.[8] In 1893, governor Roswell P. Flower again urged the New York legislature to take some action to improve the state's highways.[9] In response, the legislature offered to shift the cost of road building upward—from the towns to the counties—for towns that would agree to give up the archaic system of road maintenance by labor tax.[10] Under New York's old system, each town was divided into road districts, each of which required its male residents over the age of twenty-one to do a few days of road work each year. As Flower put it, "The people of each district naturally say, 'If the other districts will not make good roads for us, they do not deserve that we should make good roads for them, and there is but little advantage in our making such short strips of good road for ourselves.'"[11] The so-called county system replaced the labor tax with a money tax and put care of the roads in the hands of county officials, who could at least establish uniform standards of maintenance within their own counties.

New York farmers opposed using state money to pave roads because they regarded it as a way of using their taxes to subsidize the hobby of rich city folk. In 1897, when the state legislature considered a bill to eliminate the labor system of road taxation entirely, upstate legislators declared that it was "simply legislation in the interest of the bicyclists, who desired that the farmers be taxed and the money spent in improving the roads. . . . [T]he country members were a unit against it."[12] The farmers were not unjustified in their objection, given that the failed road bill had been written by the New York division of the League of American Wheelmen.[13]

The Good Roads movement failed in Wisconsin in the early 1890s for the same reason. In 1895, five years after first organizing, the Wisconsin division of the League of American Wheelmen, in conjunction with the state's merchants, got a bill before the legislature authorizing state aid for county roads, patterned on the plan of the Massachusetts Highway Commission. The state's rural legislators, convinced that the law was merely an attempt to get state money for a few wealthy city bicyclists, argued that the state's prohibition against internal improvements forbade such a measure and defeated the bill. Wisconsin did not organize a state highway commission until 1907.[14]

In 1898, New York finally passed a road bill—the Higbie-Armstrong Act—over the objections of rural representatives, who again complained that the proposal would raise their taxes. This time some rural representatives joined the urban supporters of the plan.[15] New York's Good Roads act, like the highway acts of Massachusetts and New Jersey, placed the initiative for road improvement in the hands of local, not state, officials. The Higbie-Armstrong Act allowed boards of county supervisors to request technical and financial assistance from the state to facilitate improvement of short stretches of road.[16] When county supervisors asked for such assistance, the state engineer would inspect their plans, make suggestions, and oversee the actual improvement of the road. The state paid half of the cost, the township contributed 35 percent, and the county put up the rest.[17] Rural doomsayers were exactly right about the ultimate fiscal effect of the law: The road improvements were so expensive that, even with the state footing half the bill, tax rates went up whenever a county undertook improvements under the act.[18]

By 1900, Good Roads advocates were making comparisons between their own day and the time of Henry Clay and John C. Calhoun, when the states had taken the initiative to construct roads and canals to build up trade in the young republic.[19] New York state's largest transportation initiative in the period from 1895 to 1905, the Barge Canal, seemed to support the notion that a second era of internal improvements had arrived. In 1895, instead of investing in the twentieth-century technology of paved highways, the Empire State started to rebuild its most famous nineteenth-century transportation project: the Erie Canal.

The effect of that great artificial waterway on nineteenth-century state finances cannot be overstated. The Erie Canal had a lasting impact on state finances far outside New York's borders and long after its completion in 1825. Other states were eager to copy the Empire State's success in building such a colossal public work that not only facilitated trade across the state but also made enough money to pay for itself as well as the general costs of the state government. Pennsylvania, Ohio, and Illinois all undertook similar projects, borrowing astronomical sums in the process.[20] New York also continued to build, expanding the Erie Canal with feeder canals into the hinterlands of the state. From 1817 to 1842, the state borrowed heavily to finance the canal system.[21] Then, at the height of canal enthusiasm, the Panic of 1837 struck. Several states, including Pennsylvania, were caught short and had to default on interest payments. By 1842, New York appeared to be ready to follow.[22]

The depression of the late 1830s remade state fiscal policy in the antebellum North. Just as New York had led the way by building the Erie Canal in the first place, the Empire State also established the model for coping with the situation. Clearly, internal improvements could not support the cost of state government. Nor could the state continue to borrow good money only to throw it after bad. Instead, the state had to bite the bullet, impose property taxes, and pay all expenses out of current revenue.[23] In 1842, the state stopped all canal construction and levied a property tax.[24] Other states followed New York's example. In 1843, Pennsylvania actually defaulted on its canal debt interest payments and had to sell off its canal properties. The Keystone State's pioneer 1844 corporation tax originated in that fiscal debacle.[25] Many northeastern states revised their constitutions to prohibit state borrowing for the purpose of internal improvements. New western states founded in the 1840s, including Wisconsin, Oregon, and California, adopted similar restrictions on state aid to internal improvements.[26] Those debt restrictions would have enormous consequences for the politics of public spending fifty years later, during the second era of internal improvements.

From 1842 to 1890, New York engaged almost no long-term debt. Only in 1891, when unfavorable winds and low water in Lake Erie posed a serious threat to canal navigation, did New Yorkers begin to take seriously the possibility of new internal improvements.[27] The legislature appointed a special commission to investigate the possibility of expanding the canal.[28] In the fall of 1892, a group of merchants and shippers met in Buffalo to organize a coherent set of demands for canal construction.[29] They concluded that the canal really needed significant broadening and deepening along its whole length.[30]

Pressure for canal expansion finally had a measurable effect on state politics during the state constitutional convention of 1894. One proposed amendment would have allowed the legislature to improve the canals as it saw fit, if construction were funded according to the state's debt limitation amendment or through an equitable tax. Most New Yorkers, including members of the 1895 state legislature, regarded the amendment as a litmus test of public opinion on the canals. The canal amendment passed with a larger majority than any of the convention's other proposals.[31] In response, the 1895 legislature and the voters of the state approved a referendum for a bond issue to raise $9 million for canal improvements.

The "Nine Million Bond" turned into a fiscal and political nightmare. The estimate of $9 million, which was based on a twenty-year-old survey, was much too low. By 1897 the money was gone and the work left unfinished.[32] When Republican governor Theodore Roosevelt took office in 1899, he faced the unenviable task of justifying a financial fiasco that happened on the watch of a Republican administration with a Republican legislature. He made the canals a priority, referring to them in 1900 as "the most important single State interest which is cared for directly by the State government."[33]

Roosevelt appointed two special commissions to investigate the problem. The first investigated possible criminal charges against the canal officials who were responsible for wasting the Nine Million Bond, but it found no criminal conduct.[34] The second commission considered how to finish the job begun by the Nine Million Bond. Its membership revealed the importance of the apolitical aspects of professional expertise in transportation expenditures. The commission included Francis V. Greene, who had demonstrated his organizational talents in New York City's 1889 street cleaning program; Thomas W. Symons of the U.S. Army Corps of Engineers, who had recently published a study on the feasibility of a ship canal from the Great Lakes to the Atlantic for the federal government; and the current state engineer and surveyor.[35] The professional opinions of civil engineers and canal experts, based on scientific objectivity, would protect Roosevelt's canal policies from charges of political motivation.[36]

The commission concluded that the state should at least undertake a $200,000 survey of the canal system to make accurate estimates for whatever project the voters approved. The legislature approved such a survey in 1901.[37] Between 1900 and 1902, commercial groups and engineers who had favored a large-scale barge canal during the special commission's initial survey organized several statewide conventions to publicize their plan. In the 1903 session, they succeeded in passing on to the voters a referendum measure authorizing the sale of $101 million in bonds to a build a canal of sufficient size to float 100-ton barges. The referendum passed.

The battle for the barge canal revealed the importance of direct democracy in the new corporate state. Referenda allowed elections to be decided by groups organized according to explicit self-interest in a single economic issue, rather than political parties. For example, Henry W. Hill, a Republican state senator from Erie County, placed the barge canal above party loyalty by threatening to scuttle Republican projects such as the financial tax measures of 1901 if the State Senate did not approve the barge canal measure.[38] In the general referendum election, upstate counties that were distant from the canal generally opposed the measure, despite the fact that the measure specified that any special tax necessitated by the new debt would be levied only in counties adjacent to the canal itself.[39] Railroad companies also distributed "circulars, pamphlets and other anti-canal propaganda of various kinds" at various major rail stations across the state.[40] The railroads found themselves opposing their old enemies: large, well-organized, and well-funded commercial groups such as the New York Merchants' Association and the Canal Association of Greater New York.[41]

The relative strength of economic interest groups, rather than political parties, decided the barge canal referendum. Neither Republicans nor canal advocates wanted to make the barge canal a partisan issue. Both political parties could afford to advocate expensive projects in referenda because the ultimate responsibility rested with the electorate rather than with either party.[42] By removing the parsimony of partisanship, the referendum provided an electoral mechanism that could raise state spending capacity by entire orders of magnitude.

The battle for the barge canal revolutionized New York's highway policy as well. Two years after approving $100 million for canal improvements, voters decided to issue another $50 million in bonds to pay for highway construction. The *New York Times* maintained that the "intention" of the highway bond issue was "to please the country districts offended by the canal amendment."[43] Thus, an alliance between Good Roads and barge canal advocates resulted in the Empire State's most massive transportation investments since the construction of the Erie Canal, bringing New York into the second era of internal improvements.

Between 1900 and 1916, several other states, including some Jeffersonian republics, enacted state-aid laws of smaller magnitude. In 1903, the year that New York passed its barge canal and highway system act, Pennsylvania created a centralized system of highways to be built and maintained by the state. In 1911, Alabama and Wisconsin enacted somewhat less ambitious state-aid provisions. Alabama's law authorized the state to distribute income from the state's convict-lease program to the counties for road purposes; Wisconsin established a state highway department that was responsible for maintaining a network of roads linking all of the county seats. Oregon created its highway commission in 1913 and provided for money and engineering assistance to counties.[44] None of those states, however, borrowed or spent significant amounts until the 1920s.

Debt financing was critical to the corporate states' early, large investments in transportation infrastructure. Large-scale construction projects were impossible to pay for with the relatively puny annual revenues of most states. As one historian noted, "Between 1919 and 1938 the states borrowed far more for highway purposes than they had borrowed for all purposes in the preceding one hundred and thirty years."[45] In addition, debt financing took transportation out of the realm of partisan politics by requiring approval by the voters in referenda—because of the debt limitations adopted by virtually every state constitution in the 1840s. Debt limitations required states to amend their constitutions to authorize debt issues. Constitutional amendments always required popular referenda. Therefore, constitutional debt limitations forced large-scale debt issues into electoral politics, even in states such as New York that had not yet adopted the initiative or the referendum.

The 1910 highway bond election in California, the only other state to engage in major highway spending before 1920, underscored the importance of direct democracy in freeing state capacity from the bonds of partisanship. As in New York's 1905 campaign, motorists were the major advocates of the 1910 measure in California. During the legislative session of 1909, governor James

N. Gillett met several times with the California Good Roads Association to discuss the draft of the bill. They spent most of their time arguing about the administrative structure of the new state road project. The association advocated a county-centered system like those of other states, but Gillett insisted on centralization of planning and construction at the state level.[46] The association's most vociferous advocates of a county system apparently were southern Californians whose counties already had undertaken large debts for highway construction and wanted some help after the fact.

To the Good Roads advocates, the law's most objectionable administrative feature was that it made the state engineer, not boards of county supervisors, responsible for planning the highway system. Even the state engineer himself opposed the plan, favoring instead a decentralized county road system partly funded by the state.[47] In the end, however, Gillett got his way, and the legislature approved a centralized state highway system.

In managing the bill through the legislature, the governor appealed openly to the state's agricultural interests, suggesting that it would give farmers smoother roads that would not bruise their fruit on the way to market, increase commerce and traffic, and encourage tourism.[48] The bill rolled out of the Assembly Committee on Roads and Highways with a "do pass" recommendation, to which both houses of the legislature agreed.[49]

Motorists also made significant contributions to the referendum campaign of 1910, when the measure went to the voters for final approval. On November 2, 1910, Gillett led a parade of cars into Stockton to deliver a stump speech in favor of the highway bond issue, with autos and drivers supplied by the Sacramento Automobile Club.[50] The bond issue, which the San Francisco *Chronicle* called "overwhelming in its significance as the forerunner of an era of prodigious and magnificent development," passed.[51]

California officials knew exactly what they were doing when they abrogated a half-century of debt-free financing and disengagement from public improvements. "At the present time," mused the state controller in a 1908 speech, "there are signs indicating that state governments may be pushed by public sentiment into the undertaking of enterprises of such magnitude as will require borrowing on a larger scale."[52] In recognizing the importance of "public sentiment" in "pushing" the states toward borrowing to fund transportation projects, the controller echoed the comments of other state officials during the period who remarked on the popularity of state spending programs. The spread of the initiative as an electoral reform made it even easier for the public to turn popular spending programs into fiscal reality.

Well-organized interest groups, especially motorists, quickly learned to take advantage of public eagerness for highway bond issues. The California State Automobile Association (CSAA), for example, published campaign guides for organizing highway bond elections. The CSAA recommended sending press releases to the local newspapers, filled with statistics from the U.S. Department of Agriculture's Bureau of Public Roads about the benefits of good roads. Next would come weekly or semi-weekly meetings with lantern slides, stereopticon shows, and movies of "children slipping and sliding to the one-room schoolhouse over muddy roads in comparison with children going dry-shod over paved highways to the modern union school in the modern motor bus." Having won the franchise in California in 1911, women electioneers had particularly important jobs, making telephone calls and mailing postcards to women voters, "asking them as sisters to help get good roads from the farm to town." According to the general manager of the CSAA Good Roads Bureau, women worked "harder than the men and almost invariably record[ed] a larger percentage of the vote." In fact, he dedicated his book on the Good Roads Movement in California "TO THE WOMEN OF CALIFORNIA WHO HAVE HELPED MORE THAN ANY OTHER AGENCY IN THE FIGHT FOR GOOD ROADS."[53]

In 1916, the financial incentives of the Federal Aid Road Act got the Jeffersonian republics of the South and West onboard the Good Roads bandwagon. States such as Georgia, Mississippi, and Nevada hurried to organize highway departments in 1916 and 1917 to take advantage of the Act.[54] In contrast, eastern corporate states that had already made such investments on their own benefited little from the Federal Aid Road Act. The governor of New York pointed out that states such as his, which opted out of the federal act's matching-funds provisions, still had to contribute federal taxes toward the $75 million congressional appropriation. New York's share amounted to $29 million, and the state stood to gain less than $4 million. "It is not even necessary," the governor concluded sourly, "to comment on the unfairness of this proposition."[55]

California's highway bond issue of 1919 showed how popular state highway construction had become. In February, the CSAA and the state highway commission called a meeting of the state association of county supervisors, women's clubs, chambers of commerce, and farm bureaus to convince them of the necessity of issuing another $40 million in bonds to complete the state highway system. Although the officials objected at first to "being called together to be programmed by a few paid employees of automobile associations," the meeting laid the foundation of a powerful electoral coalition.[56] Its campaign material promised to bring Californians a future of unlimited prosperity on miles of new pavement.[57] On July 1, 1919, voters approved the $40 million highway bond. In some rural counties, the bond went entirely unopposed. Business and government officials worked hand-in-glove on the campaign; in fact, the state engineer wrote the *Motor Land* article announcing the victory.[58]

Although California and New York were ahead of the curve, after 1920 the states played an important role in building the country's new highway system.[59] In 1904, the states had contributed only 4 percent of the nation's total highway expenditures; ten years later, their share had grown to 10 percent; by 1926, the states had shouldered 38 percent, and in 1930 the states' share of total highway expenditures in the United States reached 53 percent.[60] State expenditures therefore were crucial to the second era of internal improvements, especially during the construction boom of the 1920s.

The first World War put many functions of state government on hold from 1917 through 1920. Construction projects in particular suffered from shortages and inflated prices for materials and labor. In 1918, for example, the New York comptroller reported that highway construction in his state had been "virtually abandoned" during the war.[61] Many state officials considered highway construction a key element in the problem of "Reconstruction," the return to normalcy of the 1920s. In 1921, various state and municipal emergency groups met to promote public improvement projects as a means of ending the painful postwar recession. Simultaneously, a new federal road appropriation also encouraged state highway construction.[62]

Even during a period when state spending expanded in all directions, the growth of transportation expenditures was dramatic. In 1902, total expenditures by all states for all purposes amounted to about $2.47 for each man, woman, and child in the United States. In 1927, the states collectively spent (in 1902 dollars) just more than $8.26 per person. Thus, total state spending in 1927 was about three times what it had been in 1902. During the same period, state spending on highways increased by a factor of thirty-nine, climbing from a nickel per person to $2.07. Highway expenditures grew from just 2 percent of total state expenditures to 25 percent.[63] By the late 1920s, virtually every state devoted a significant share of its annual expenditures to highways.[64] As the director of the National Automobile Chamber of Commerce remarked in 1926, "The demands of 18,000,000 motor vehicles make highway improvements one of the primary functions of the state government—than which it has no more important use for its funds."[65]

With its enormous investments in canal and highway construction, New York stood out from the rest of the states as an early investor in transportation, devoting more than 40 percent of total state expenditures to transportation in the peak year of 1913. Other states eventually approached those heights, but not until the late 1920s. The early highway commission states, such as Massachusetts and New Jersey, actually devoted only a small share of total state expenditures to transportation until after 1917.

The highway spending boom of the 1920s had the most dramatic impact on the Jeffersonian republics of the South, the Great Plains, and the West. Those states spent virtually nothing on transportation until after 1916, when highway spending exploded. Tennessee and Illinois devoted almost half of their annual expenditures to transportation by 1928. In 1923, transportation expenditures in Nevada accounted for more than 60 percent of total state spending.

Those spending patterns differed sharply from the slow, steady growth of state spending before 1900. In terms of actual dollar amounts, only Massachusetts took an incremental approach to building highways.[66] Every other state invested in highways in sudden bursts. Where state spending curves for education and health care look like gentle hills, the charts of state transportation spending look like stair steps or jagged cliffs. Where spending on schools and asylums before 1900 was incremental, spending on highways after 1915 was nonincremental. Capital-intensive construction projects required enormous funds up front, so states that wanted roads had to pay right away. Except for the early highway commission states—such as New York, New Jersey, and Pennsylvania—virtually every state spent practically nothing on highways until after 1917, when they suddenly elevated transportation to an importance previously reserved for education.

In the second era of internal improvements, a political reshaping of state fiscal capacities also remade the American physical landscape. Between 1904 and 1925, the states built half a million miles of new roads, linking isolated farms to towns, taking children to school, getting motorists out of the mud, speeding up the wheelmen's rides, and performing all of the thousand little miracles preached by the Good Roads movement and the automobile associations.[67] The political process that built those roads changed American government almost as much as the roads changed the landscape. Between 1890 and 1929, the rise of direct democracy dramatically increased state fiscal capacity. Interest groups, not parties, fought those elections, so parties had no incentive to keep spending down to stay in office. The initiative and the referendum were necessary institutional preconditions for interest groups to operate. More than any other kind of election, bond issue referenda organized voters on the basis of their economic self-interest instead of their political party. These referenda were a critical factor in the shift from the participatory, partisan, distributive state of the nineteenth century to the pluralist, administrative, corporate state of the twentieth century.[68]

In addition to the fundamental change in American politics wrought by the spread of the initiative and the referendum, the political aspects of highway construction altered state fiscal policy by placing sudden and extreme strains on state finances. Unlike the incremental growth of school and asylum spending before 1900, the nonincremental expenditures required for highway construction created heavy debt loads and demanded new solutions to the old fiscal problems of state taxation.

Highway expenditures piled up on top of the states' existing commitments to care for the insane and educate children. Even as states plunged enthusiastically into ambitious road construction programs, they continued to expand the services they offered to school children and to maintain a minimum level of care for mentally disabled people. Whatever the Automobile Chamber of Commerce said, new highway spending did not replace the states' existing mission of educating children and caring for the insane. Instead, it added new layers of fiscal responsibility. The combination of sudden growth in transportation spending and continued steady growth in education and hospital spending forced states to revolutionize their entire financial systems.

FIVE

Consent, Control, and Centralization

SCHOOL AND HOSPITAL SPENDING, 1900 TO 1929

As horses and buggies gave way to automobiles and graded gravel roads replaced wagon-wheel ruts, less visible but equally important changes were
transforming public education and mental health care. Twentieth-century
progress demanded more than the simple goal of free elementary education for
every child. Progressive states introduced union high schools, teacher training,
free textbooks, and buses to drive children to school on the new state roads.
In the teacher shortage that followed the first World War, corporate states offered financial aid to smaller towns and counties to supplement teacher salaries
and attract qualified candidates. In the field of mental health care, nineteenth-
century insane asylums, with their barred windows and locked doors, were
gradually replaced by mental hospitals with open wards, operating rooms, and
pathological laboratories. New treatments, such as electric shock therapy and
surgical sterilization, seemed to be full of promise.

These developments were only the visible changes. Even more significant
were the underlying administrative and financial trends that made those innovations possible. Two of the most important of those trends continued to distinguish high-spending corporate states from minimalist Jeffersonian republics.
First, the nature of disinterested expertise changed profoundly. Genteel reformers such as Frank Sanborn lost credibility. In their place, medical doctors

with psychiatric training took control of state mental health agencies. Second, a similar change reformulated the definition of adequate education. Local school systems were increasingly brought under statewide standards for curriculum, teacher training, and physical plant. Those changes had particularly important implications for states with large rural constituencies because the result usually was imposition of urban systems on rural schools.

Those two trends did not alter the basic pattern of institutional change in state government, in which nonpartisan experts—usually state employees themselves—acted as driving agents of policy change. Initiatives and referenda also remained important in freeing large expenditures from the stigma of partisanship. Political contingency still mattered as well. Particular events or issues in each state affected developments in education and mental health care.

Innovations in mental health care and education tended to centralize authority at the state level, which meant raising state spending. That trend was evident in the Northeast, the Midwest, and the Far West and to a lesser extent in the Great Plains. In contrast, southern state governments continued to offer few services in either area. In the South, health care and education were developed during this period not by state governments but by northeastern philanthropic institutions such as the Rockefeller Fund. In combination with radical, nonincremental spending increases in transportation, the steady progress of education and health care in the corporate states ultimately demanded modernization of state tax systems as well.

Around the end of the nineteenth century, the definition of medical expertise in mental health care shifted from practical experience in charity work to university-level medical and scientific research and training. In 1892, the Association of Medical Superintendents of American Institutions for the Insane (AMSAII) recognized that shift by changing its name to the American Medico-Psychological Association and changing its mission statement to include research into all kinds of diseases.[1] The continuing specialization of psychiatry changed the minimum qualifications for government officials in charge of state mental health systems. Earlier in the nineteenth century, it had been enough to appoint a few men and women of good character, such as Frank Sanborn or Louisa Schuyler, to a board of charities and corrections. Those genteel reformers spent their time visiting each of the state's various institutions to make sure the patients were being well treated. By the 1890s, however, that approach was no longer sufficient. The new state boards, such as New York's Commission in Lunacy, had to be staffed by professionals of the same caliber as the directors of the state's mental hospitals. In addition, the new agencies had to wield centralized managerial authority over the entire system of state asylums.[2] The victory of New York's State Care Act in 1890 was not only a victory for the State Charities Aid Association and, its members hoped, for mentally afflicted New Yorkers. It also was a victory for the Commission in Lunacy and its new style of professional control. As Sanborn remarked disapprovingly in 1903, the New York Commission in Lunacy had "centralized and *personified* (so to speak) the care of the insane of New York."[3]

Reformers had argued about which method of state management was better since the 1870s. Should states adopt a management approach that was based on consent, like the old boards of charities and corrections, or an approach that was based on control, like New York's Lunacy Commission?[4] Should the duties of the state board consist merely of visitation and friendly advice, or should the board have ultimate control over hiring, firing, and management of the institutions it oversaw? The new standards of psychiatric expertise pushed states toward the latter option.

In 1898, for example, the Massachusetts Board of Lunacy and Charity, whose powers had been deliberately reduced by lunacy reformers such as Sanborn in 1879, recommended the creation of a new and more powerful agency than itself. The existing board recommended that the new State Board of Insanity be staffed by "medical experts" and given "complete control" over classification and care of the state's mentally ill.[5]

In response to the Board of Lunacy and Charity's recommendation, the state legislature established the new Board of Insanity in 1898, requiring that two of its members be doctors and empowering it to make decisions for the state's entire insane population. The members of the new board interpreted their legislative mandate to be development of a statewide system for care of the insane. They recommended that care of the insane be removed entirely from the counties, shifting a significant financial burden to the state.[6] In yet another demonstration of the importance of nonpartisan expertise in the development of state capacity, the 1900 legislature complied with this recommendation, making it illegal for any locality to care for an insane person after 1904.[7]

The 1900 law committed the state to supporting and treating its insane population but did not specify what form that care and treatment would take. Sanborn hoped it would take the form of a system of small cottages and family-type accommodations instead of the "great state asylums" to which the insane were relegated in New York, which he considered "an injustice, even an injury, to the insane."[8] He was to be disappointed. In 1902, the state approved the issue of more than half a million dollars of scrip to fund the construction of additions to its existing facilities. As the state auditor put it, the intent was "to provide more economically for the annual increase in the number of insane by providing for increasing the capacity of the existing hospitals rather than to establish any new institutions."[9]

The cost was still enormous. When the law took effect in 1904, it increased the state's annual operating expenses by $1.1 million at a time when the state's current expenses (not counting redemption of debt or transfer payments) amounted to only $9.6 million a year.[10] The cost of state care for the insane was so high that it prompted governor John L. Bates to call for a higher property tax or some other new source of revenue to pay for it.[11]

Unlike most states, Massachusetts lacked a constitutional prohibition against state indebtedness. This unique institutional factor allowed the Bay State to issue scrip and bonds through the legislature without referring such measures to a general election. As a result, virtually every measure that Massachusetts passed could be claimed by (or blamed on) one party or the other. In 1905, Republicans made a virtue of necessity and tried to turn the large expenditures to their own advantage. In *The New England Republican Primer . . . to which is Added the Republican Catechism, Etc.*—a political pamphlet distributed in that year—Republicans published this "catechism": "Q. What State does the most to care for its Insane? A. Massachusetts, under Republican administration. Q. What does this cost? A. $1,100,000 was expended by the State this year solely for the care of the insane, formerly paid for directly by cities and towns. Q. Why was this done? A. To give them the best of care. Q. Is this extravagance? A. Certainly not."[12]

In 1905, Governor Bates's lieutenant governor, Curtis Guild Jr., was elected governor in his own right. In his inaugural speech, Guild reminded the legislature that the state had relieved the localities of more than $1 million a year in taxes, without making any provisions for recovering that cost at the state level. Guild even went so far as to ask for a revision of the corporation tax to pay for the asylums, suggesting that the state take a larger share of the corporation tax revenue and distribute less to the localities.[13] The legislature rejected that idea, and the costs of state care of the insane continued to mount. In 1909, when the state took over the hospital in Boston, the legislature had to authorize a $1 million bond issue to fund it.[14]

Guild exemplified the new generation of Progressive Republican politicians who took an interest in tax reform in the early twentieth century. Wealthy and well-connected, Guild came from a business background. His father had founded the *Boston Commercial Bulletin,* and after a successful career at Harvard (where he honed his editing skills on the *National Lampoon*), the younger Guild took over the family paper. During the Spanish-American War, Guild served as first lieutenant and adjutant-general of the Sixth Massachusetts Infantry Volunteers, earning a promotion to lieutenant colonel and inspector general of Havana. In 1900, Guild toured the West with his new friend, Theodore Roosevelt, on the Rough Rider's vice presidential campaign. Guild's political career continued as lieutenant governor and then governor of Massachusetts. At the 1908 Republican nominating convention, he was briefly considered as a running mate for William Howard Taft.[15]

Guild had an abiding interest in tax reform because progress was forcing him to raise taxes. As governor, he asked the legislature repeatedly to change the corporation tax so that the state could retain a larger share, to no avail.[16] His biggest tax reform success in Massachusetts was the passage of an inheritance tax measure in 1908.[17] In 1907, Guild was one of the central figures in the founding of the single most influential tax organization in twentieth-century America, the National Tax Association. As chairman of the NTA's first meeting, Guild recommended that the new group's first priority be the drafting of a model income tax law.[18]

As governor of Massachusetts, Guild faced the unenviable task of assimilating an enormously expensive new program without a source of additional funding. Under the property tax regime, higher expenditures translated directly into higher taxes. As a Massachusetts state legislative commission remarked in 1907, "The expenses of the State have reached such an amount and are soon to reach such a larger amount that new sources of revenue are imperative."[19] Tax officials and politicians in the same position as Guild made the same complaint throughout the nation. The situation eventually (in 1916) drove Massachusetts to join the income tax revolution.

In the field of mental health care, new definitions of professional authority centralized administrative authority in New York and Massachusetts. The movement from consent to control took the shape of statewide systems of large insane asylums, which demanded large shares of public expenditures to build and maintain. In both cases, the role of medical professionals in state government was a crucial determinant in the timing of state adoption of care of the mentally ill population.

In 1897, California started on a similar path. In that year, governor James H. Budd asked the state legislature to create a central supervisory agency with the power to guarantee uniform commitment and accounting procedures. Budd wanted to reduce the number of "commitments . . . made for the purpose of ridding the county of some harmless nuisance." He also wanted to be able to consult "uniform books." In fact, he thought New York's asylum system worked so well that he recommended that the legislature simply adopt the same language, "amended to meet the requirements of our state."[20] The 1897 legislature heeded Budd's request and created the California Commission in Lunacy.

The California agency was much less powerful than its Empire State counterpart. The California commission was composed of the governor, the secretary of state, and the attorney general (who together made up the state board of examiners, a kind of primitive budgetary oversight committee); the secretary of the State Board of Health; and only a single new official, the general superintendent of state hospitals.[21] As the commissioners put it in their first report, the 1897 law renamed asylums "state hospitals, and the Lunacy Commission was given a confirmatory power over the actions of the State hospital management."[22]

After the wave of state-level consolidations of mental hospitals around the turn of the twentieth century, few states made any real changes in mental health policy until the 1920s. Most states merely added more beds when they could, but the first two decades of the twentieth century generally were a period of stagnation. In California, for example, money got so tight in the 1910s that the attorney for the Commission in Lunacy spent much of his time tracking down deadbeat families who refused to support their relatives in the state asylum.[23] Partly to relieve the crowding, the Golden State inaugurated a system of "psychopathic parole" in 1913, which allowed institutions to place less dangerous inmates under the care of a "psychopathic parole officer" and enabled those inmates to live outside the hospital.[24]

The first World War hit state hospitals hard. Already overcrowded and understaffed throughout the 1910s, state mental hospitals had to scramble to find even unqualified help during the war years. As the Massachusetts Commission on Mental Diseases noted in 1919, "It is no longer a question of selecting properly qualified employees from applications, but taking everyone available, and even then falling far short of the required quota."[25] The war had a double impact on New York's mental hospitals. After drawing away funding and staff and forcing officials to defer maintenance, it brought a flood of new shell-shock cases into already crowded institutions.[26] With an institutional population growing at the rate of almost 700 per year, the state's mental hospitals were desperately overcrowded by the end of the war.[27]

A horrific event in 1923 galvanized the Empire State into doing something about its crumbling mental hospitals. At 5:20 A.M. on Sunday, February 18, the head night attendant in Ward 43 of the Manhattan State Hospital on Ward's Island saw the lights go out above his post in the fourth-floor hallway. Moments later, he saw the tin ceiling starting to glow red, and he sounded the fire alarm. Ward 43 held the hospital's most dangerous and deranged patients, many of whom were considered homicidal or suicidal. As attendants rushed to get them out of their rooms, some clung to their beds, and others "roared with laughter at the flame and confusion and broke into tears when they were forced to leave a scene calculated to delight lunatics of the pyromaniac and excitement-thirsting types."[28]

Outside, the temperature was seven degrees above zero. Thick sheets of ice encrusted the building as the Ward's Island Fire Department played their hoses over the burning building. Sixty-three of the eighty-five patients in the ward had been hustled to safety in the cafeteria when the five-and-a-half ton water tank on the roof fell through the burning attic and into the fourth-floor corridor. Three attendants and twenty-two patients died in the fire. Three of the patients were veterans with shell-shock. It was the worst disaster ever to strike the New York state hospital system.[29]

Dr. Marcus B. Heyman, the hospital superintendent, blamed the high number of fatalities on overcrowding, dilapidated buildings, and inadequate firefighting equipment. The cause of the blaze was never determined, although investigators ruled out faulty wiring and suspected that someone had dropped a match or lit cigarette into a heating vent.[30] Ironically, a week earlier, Heyman had spoken with governor Alfred E. Smith about increased funding for the state hospitals; improving the hospital system had been one of Smith's campaign planks in the previous fall's election.[31] On February 22, Smith asked the legislature to send a $50 million bond issue to the voters at the next election to build new facilities and fireproof the old ones.[32] The legislature passed the measure.

As the referendum went to the polls, Smith and the state hospital commission campaigned vigorously. In their electioneering, they enlisted the support of a variety of voluntary associations, including the YMCA; the Merchants' Association of New York City; the Buffalo, Ogdensburg, and Brooklyn Chambers of Commerce; and the New York State Charities Aid Association.[33] Columbia University president Nicholas Murray Butler declared the hospital bond issue among the three most critical questions to be decided in that year's election.[34] The bond issue passed by a margin of almost three to one.[35]

The hospital bond measure of 1923 proved as significant in the fiscal history of New York as the Barge Canal measure two decades earlier. In 1925, voters approved another bond issue, this time for $100 million, for the purpose of improving state buildings. Together with the 1923 hospital bond issue, the 1925 construction measure inaugurated what state officials called "a new era in the history of the state debt."[36] From 1777, when the New York state government was founded, to 1925, when the first hospital bonds were sold, the state had built all of its public buildings with current revenues. The hospital bonds ended 150 years of "pay-as-you-go" financing for state buildings. New York's mental health care system had become so large that it finally forced the state to adopt modern methods of debt financing to keep up its physical plant.

The shift from consent to control in state mental health care created nonincremental patterns in hospital expenditures in several states besides Massachusetts and New York.[37] As one would expect, Massachusetts' state-care program between 1900 and 1909 drove up hospital spending dramatically, from about twenty-five cents per capita to more than $1.40. New Jersey and Michigan also ratcheted up hospital spending, doubling their spending figures from 1900 to 1928.

Mississippi deviated from the southern pattern of minimal or, at best, incremental state spending by raising its hospital expenditures from a few cents per capita in 1901 to more than fifty cents by 1928. In contrast, other southern states kept their hospital expenditures low. Although northern philanthropic agencies such as the Rockefeller Sanitary Commission spread public health programs across the South in the first decades of the twentieth century, dispensary programs and hookworm eradication campaigns seem to have had little effect on spending for state mental hospitals.[38] Per capita hospital spending in the Great Plains and Far West differed greatly from state to state. Kansas retained a pattern of incremental growth, and hospital spending in California and Oregon actually declined.

Progressive states were characterized by a shift from consent to control in the field of mental health care; they also were marked by a strong trend toward centralization in the field of education. In education, standardization and consolidation were the watchwords between the turn of the twentieth century and the first World War. President Theodore Roosevelt's Country Life Commission of 1908 drew national attention to the ramshackle conditions of most rural schools and the lack of opportunities for many farm children. Many townships solved their funding problems by consolidating several far-flung schools into union schools. In the cities, teaching lurched toward professionalization as trained administrators gradually replaced politically appointed ward heelers as superintendents. Counties and states began to publish standards for public schools, using funding as a carrot to encourage schools to adopt modern practices.[39]

In the South, twentieth-century educational reform began with the Southern Education Board (SEB), founded in 1901 by New York businessman Robert C. Ogden. With assistance from John D. Rockefeller Jr., the SEB campaigned for state-level educational reform throughout the South. The SEB scored major successes in organizing the Summer School of the South in Knoxville, Tennessee, which educated teachers and school administrators in summer programs from 1902 through 1907. In 1909, reformers convinced the Tennessee legislature to pass a law that significantly raised state expenditures for public schools, followed by a compulsory attendance law in 1913.[40]

In the West, efforts to standardize school curriculum also accounted for growing education spending between 1901 and the first World War. In 1903, for example, California adopted a system of standard, state-approved textbooks, and in 1912 it committed state money to provide them to all students at no charge.[41] The same year, the Golden State finally devoted state money to public high schools, at the rate of $15 per student.[42]

New Yorkers discovered that rural school reform was more complicated than issuing legislative fiats from Albany. In 1917, New York passed a law facilitating consolidation of small rural districts into larger units. The state department of education, the law's major sponsor, justified the measure on the grounds of equalizing educational opportunities for rural children.[43] Outraged farmers, whom the department of education had not bothered to consult in drafting the law, had their representatives repeal it in 1918.[44]

The first World War affected schools the same way it affected hospitals and highways: It diverted resources and labor from all sectors of state activity. Postwar "reconstruction," as New York governor Al Smith declared in 1919, posed "problems of finance and banking, as well as the questions of sanitation, unemployment, labor, the position of women in industry, education and military training, [which] need[ed] solution as peace measures."[45] In the wake of the teacher shortage caused by the war, states scrambled to find warm bodies to stand in front of chalkboards.

In the 1920s, education spending grew across the board. The most significant change was the growth of state aid to local schools.[46] Massachusetts, for example, departed from its longstanding policy of local school funding. In 1918 the state legislature passed a law setting a minimum salary of $550 for teachers. Because the law had no state appropriation attached, however, it amounted to little more than an unfunded mandate. Nevertheless, local school districts responded with a general raise for the Commonwealth's teachers. In 1919 the legislature actually appropriated $4 million to subsidize teacher salaries, especially in "towns of low valuation." According to Massachusetts officials, the law was supposed to equalize opportunity for rural and urban children. The subsidies had prevented any early school closures during even the worst teacher shortages of 1920. Only when the "smaller communities," which had the most trouble attracting teachers during and immediately after the war, could offer teacher salaries commensurate with those in larger towns would rural children attain equal educational opportunity.[47]

Oregon's teacher shortage in 1920 was so severe that the Portland Chamber of Commerce adopted a resolution asking other chambers of commerce and commercial clubs throughout the state to help campaign for higher teacher salaries.[48] The same problem prompted California teachers' unions and the state superintendent of public instruction to campaign for a state constitutional amendment authorizing larger distributions of the state school fund and higher salaries for teachers. Teachers, like other interest groups involved in the new pluralist politics of the initiative and referendum system, took their case directly to the voters. The California Teachers' Association began to circulate petitions for an initiative that would amend the state constitution to allow a higher state contribution to school districts and require school districts to devote at least 60 percent of their annual expenditures to teacher salaries. In another example of state officials using their position to advance basic policy changes, state superintendent Will C. Wood wrote propaganda and helped organize the campaign.[49] The amendment passed by a wide margin. Like Massachusetts, California raised its contributions to local school districts to counteract the effects of the first World War on the labor supply and to correct a decade-long slide in the real salaries of teachers.

In 1925, New York took another try at improving school conditions in rural counties. After the wartime teacher shortage had subsided, New York finally succeeded in passing a district consolidation law. Under the leadership of upstate representative Ernest E. Cole, a former teacher, the legislature approved a set of four school laws. The first law set aside $9 million to increase the state's direct contributions to school districts in proportion to need, so that the poorest districts would receive the most assistance. The most significant feature of the other "Cole Acts" consisted of incentives to dissolve tiny old school districts and create larger unified school districts. In exchange for creating unified

TABLE 2. Annual Common School Spending from All Sources and Percentage of School Revenues from Local Taxes, Selected States and Years, 1906 to 1930

	1906		1911		1916		1920		1926		1930	
	Total	Local Tax	Total	Local Tax	Total	Local Tax	Total	Local Tax	Total	Local Tax	Total	Local Tax
East												
Massachusetts	$5.43	97%	$5.75	96%	$5.65	97%	$4.42	88%	$8.78	92%	$9.97	91%
New York	$5.78	67%	$4.91	87%	$5.15	80%	$4.25	88%	$10.14	79%	$14.52	71%
New Jersey	$4.00	67%	$6.06	83%	$6.82	52%	$5.40	64%	$11.86	79%	$14.70	79%
Pennsylvania	$3.93	64%	$4.73	59%	$5.57	90%	$3.51	83%	$8.68	85%	$9.46	86%
South												
Tennessee	$1.42	64%	$2.03	77%	$2.28	81%	$1.81	82%	$3.88	76%	$4.32	76%
Alabama	$0.68	28%	$1.51	27%	$1.65	38%	$1.62	47%	$3.25	62%	$4.06	57%
Mississippi	$1.02	16%	$1.31	41%	$1.14	38%	$1.27	39%	$3.11	66%	$4.31	67%
Midwest												
Illinois	$4.40	89%	$4.70	94%	$5.50	87%	$4.46	91%	$9.14	93%	$10.10	96%
Michigan	$3.36	67%	$4.69	47%	$6.06	62%	$5.42	81%	$10.78	79%	$12.54	80%
Wisconsin	$3.56	66%	$4.19	71%	$5.13	76%	$4.31	95%	$7.66	90%	$9.10	84%
Great Plains												
North Dakota	$5.51	68%	$7.47	94%	$7.88	70%	$8.30	98%	$10.19	63%	$11.90	98%
South Dakota	$3.82	82%	$4.92	83%	$6.33	74%	$7.59	99%	$10.70	99%	$10.94	99%
Nebraska	$4.31	66%	$5.84	88%	$6.55	81%	$6.61	99%	$10.34	99%	$9.72	99%
Kansas	$3.37	88%	$5.21	91%	$6.47	97%	$6.18	99%	$9.19	99%	$10.18	99%
Far West												
Nevada	$3.61	36%	$6.26	52%	$5.52	54%	$7.45	85%	$10.84	86%	$15.22	87%
Oregon	$4.09	82%	$7.27	86%	$6.18	86%	$5.32	99%	$10.14	84%	$10.38	99%
California	$5.19	54%	$7.08	72%	$8.41	70%	$5.96	81%	$13.59	79%	$13.71	75%

SOURCE: Calculated by the author based on U.S. Department of the Interior, *Report of the Commissioner of Education* (Washington, D.C.: GPO), selected years.
NOTE: Total school spending is shown in real dollars per capita. All figures are for school years ending in the spring of the indicated calendar year. "N/A" indicates that data were not included in the Report of the Commissioner of Education. A dash indicates that the state had not yet entered the Union.

districts, the state promised to subsidize a quarter of the actual cost of building the new unified schoolhouses and half the cost of busing students there.[50] Here, at last, were educational administration laws that were acceptable to rural New Yorkers. Not only did they provide reasonable compensation for the inconvenience of sending one's children to school farther from home, they also provided immediate financial assistance with the burden of local school taxes.

Table 2 illustrates the general trend of total education spending between 1906 and 1929. Combined expenditures from all sources remained largely stable from 1906 to 1916, then plunged in 1920, in part because of drastic inflation during the war years. After 1920 total education spending shot back up, reflecting widespread new investments in education. In states such as New York, Tennessee, and Oregon, the percentage of school revenues supplied by localities fell while overall spending grew between 1920 and 1930, reflecting higher state-level expenditures. The growth of local contributions to education in the South marked a major improvement from their late-nineteenth-century overreliance on state-level funding. The share of local funding also increased in the Midwest and the Far West, although the Great Plains states continued their tradition of paying for schools entirely at the local level.

Detailed state-level spending figures reflected similar overall patterns.[51] Between 1900 and 1920, most states continued their nineteenth-century incremental spending increases. In the early 1920s, when postwar teacher salary initiatives and local-aid measures took effect, education spending rose sharply. That trend characterized education spending in New York, Pennsylvania, Michigan, Oregon, California, Tennessee, Mississippi, and Alabama. The jump in New Jersey's school expenditures reflected the railroad tax hike of 1906, followed by wartime cuts in all state programs.

In the South, education spending, like highway spending, marked the departure of many southern states from the Jeffersonian ideal of hands-off government. In states where state education spending took off, per capita dollar amounts almost equaled the sums devoted to transportation during the highway spending boom of the 1920s. In the Great Plains and the Midwest, however, Jeffersonian republics such as Illinois, Kansas, and Nebraska persisted in their nineteenth-century incremental spending patterns.

During the first three decades of the twentieth century, trends toward centralized control over state mental health and education systems raised spending on those items in almost every state, especially after 1920. In some cases, such as Massachusetts' assumption of state care for the insane in 1904 or the postwar teacher salary campaigns of California and Oregon, mental health or education even took precedence over the fiscal juggernaut of highway construction. The timing and size of investment in education and mental health care distinguished the corporate states from the Jeffersonian republics. Indeed, many states with Jeffersonian characteristics, such as Tennessee, departed dramatically from their old incremental spending patterns with relatively large investments in education and mental health.

Increasing demand for public services seemed to be forcing the states to step in. "The plain fact seems to be," explained a New York legislative commission, "that the cost of the things which the state has delegated to the local political subdivisions has increased more rapidly than the capacity of the local revenue system to expand." The commission concluded that "the taxes which should be used to raise additional funds are for the most part taxes whose successful administration demands that they be state rather than local taxes."[52] The commission was referring, of course, to the income tax.

Giants of History

INCOME AND GASOLINE TAXATION, 1907 TO 1929

By 1907, governor Curtis Guild Jr. of Massachusetts was not the only state official with a cash-flow problem. Rising costs of city and county government continued to plague New Yorkers.[1] In California, as late as 1902, the state legislature had deliberately levied an insufficient property tax to cover the state's biennial expenses, leading to extraordinarily high taxes in 1903 and 1904.[2] A slew of states, including New York and California as well as Kansas, appointed special commissions to reform their tax systems. In 1907, many of the experts and officials who contributed to those tax commissions also attended the first meeting of the most significant organization in the history of modern American taxation, the National Tax Association. Under Guild's direction, the first meeting of the NTA turned its attention to the fundamental innovation of twentieth-century taxation: the income tax.

Three basic trends combined to cause the most progressive states to adopt general or corporation income taxes between 1907 and 1929. First, independent experts from outside government, mainly academic economists, developed a coherent theory of income and corporation taxation that made sense to voters and state officials. Second, rising expenditures simply overloaded the fiscal capacity of the old property tax. Third, political struggles among various interest groups—especially financial, utility, and manufacturing firms—pushed and pulled each state's income tax system into its final shape.

Another innovation of the 1910s, the gasoline tax, also contributed to the revolution in state fiscal systems between 1907 and 1929. Jeffersonian republics and corporate states turned to the gas tax to finance their expensive new highway systems, but the gas tax ultimately was more important to the former group of states. Corporate states, such as New York and California, invested early in highways and paid for them with property or corporation taxes. In contrast, states that waited until the 1920s funded their bond issues with gasoline taxes. In those states, gasoline tax revenues dwarfed virtually all other receipts.

Income and gasoline taxes achieved a revolution sought by tax reformers since 1871. They also changed government administration in ways undreamed of by their Progressive authors. Tax reform theory, state spending, and political contingency all played a role in that revolution, but their significance differed from state to state. Before turning to the question of why individual states developed the taxes they did, I look first at the underlying factor of tax reform theory, which was common to all states that sent representatives to the NTA.

If David Wells personified tax reform in the late nineteenth century, Edwin Robert Anderson Seligman played the same role for the next generation. No other tax official or scholar could claim to have influenced modern taxation more than Seligman. The leading tax expert of his time, Seligman either formulated or popularized literally every significant theory about tax reform between 1890 and 1930. His career traced the entire arc of tax reform theory, from property tax to income taxation.

Born just a few days after the start of the Civil War in 1861, Seligman was named for the Union officer in charge of Fort Sumter, Robert Anderson. His father, a wealthy New York banker, wanted him in the family business like his brother, Isaac, but Edwin chose instead to study economics. After graduating from college in the United States, Seligman—like many economists of his generation—went to Germany to seek his doctorate. In 1884 he returned to take a teaching post at Columbia University.[3] As a more liberal member of Seligman's cohort recalled, the German-educated economists "were regarded as a group of young rebels" when they got back to the United States.[4] They returned from Germany inspired by the notion that government intervention could overcome the laws of classical economics.[5] They soon found themselves at odds with the old guard of laissez-faire theorists—including David Wells, who thought government interference would only wreck the economy.

In his work on taxation, Seligman took up where Wells had left off, publishing articles and books on every phase of the subject. The most important ideas for the future of the corporate state were the concepts of taxation based on ability to pay and separation of revenues. Taxation based on ability to pay—the "faculty theory of taxation"—was the idea that people should be taxed according to their ability to contribute. Those with the power to contribute more should be made to do so. That idea was a departure from the old "benefit theory" of taxation, which held that those with the most property benefited the most from a state that protected private property, and therefore they should pay the most.[6] Separation of revenues was the idea that state and local government should be funded from entirely separate sources. Some activities, such as transportation and transmission, were statewide, whereas some, such as manufacturing, were local. The theory held that statewide activities should be taxed at the state level, and purely local activities should be taxed by local officials.[7]

Seligman's first opportunity to apply his theoretical expertise came in 1899, when New York governor Theodore Roosevelt sought his opinion on the Ford franchise tax bill.[8] Seligman approved of the bill, which defined the right to lay pipes, wires, and tracks in city streets as a form of property called a "special franchise" and made that form of property subject to taxation at local rates. The following year, Seligman served as special consultant to the state tax committee that was called together to consider what new measures the state could take to meet its desperate need for revenue.[9]

In 1907, as a member of the New York State Tax Commission, Seligman announced proudly that the state had achieved full separation of revenues: It was paying the entire expenses of the state government out of "indirect" or corporation taxes, and property taxes were going entirely to localities.[10] In 1915, he read a speech to the NTA's annual meeting recommending that New York state adopt income taxation. Indeed, he served as consultant to the state tax commission that designed and recommended the Empire State's income tax law, which ultimately was approved in 1917.[11]

By attending the NTA's annual meetings or reading its proceedings, tax officials nationwide could learn about the faculty theory of taxation and the idea of separation of revenue. Those reform ideas contributed a theoretical basis for tax reform that all states shared. Some states, obviously—such as Seligman's New York and Guild's Massachusetts—had the advantage of being able to call on the NTA's leading experts whenever the legislature needed a little help. In most states, the NTA's basic ideas and model legislation were widely

accepted as the most progressive and up-to-date recommendations about taxation.[12]

The faculty theory of taxation and the notion of separation of revenue were
fundamental to the income tax revolution of the 1910s, but state expenditures
and the relative political power of different interest groups also affected the direction of each particular state's tax reform movement. Comparison of tax
policies adopted by California, Wisconsin, New York, and Kansas suggests
that none of those factors was sufficient in itself to cause any state to adopt income or corporation taxation; all three factors—reform theory, high state
spending, and corporate politics—had to be present for a state to join the income tax revolution.

Income taxation, of course, was not new to the United States in 1907. States
had taxed corporate incomes since the earliest railroad tax acts of the nineteenth century. Such taxes, often known as "gross receipts taxes," levied a
small percentage against a firm's total annual income. States also had experi-
mented with other forms of income taxation, especially during the Civil War,
but most of those measures, like the federal income tax of 1863, had lapsed in
the 1870s.[13] By the 1890s most tax officials, especially in the Northeast, would
have agreed with the 1893 New York Tax Commission's characterization of
income taxes as "a last resort, a kind of war measure."[14] On the other hand,
westerners and southerners would have disagreed; their congressional representatives, in fact, had approved a federal income tax that very year. In the depression year of 1893, when Populism was on the rise, a federal income tax
obviously would have redistributed national wealth from the Northeast to the
West and South. The U.S. Supreme Court agreed with the New York Tax Commission, however, and struck down the federal income tax before it could take
effect.

At its first meeting in 1907, the NTA discussed income taxation extensively.
NTA economists and state officials such as Guild, Seligman, Wisconsin's
Thomas S. Adams, and California's Carl C. Plehn pursued the income tax
agenda at the local and state levels. In 1909, the federal government imposed
a corporation income tax as part of the Payne-Aldrich Tariff. Imposed at a rate
of just 1 percent, the tax introduced no real innovations that were not already
used in various state "gross receipts" corporation taxes. The measure probably was more important as a tactic to delay passage of a general income tax
and as a thinly disguised entering wedge for regulatory reporting requirements.
At the state level, in 1910 California imposed an income-based corporation
tax that NTA officials hailed as the most perfect example of state tax reform

to date. A year later, Wisconsin levied the nation's first twentieth-century state income tax. In 1913 the federal government, authorized by the Sixteenth Amendment to the U.S. Constitution, followed suit. New York did not impose an income tax until 1917, and Kansas did not adopt one until 1933.[15]

California's 1910 tax reform bridged the nineteenth-century corporation tax and the twentieth-century income tax. Like its nineteenth-century precursors, the California tax law of 1910 originated in the crisis of the property tax. Except for the corporation license fee of 1905, California had imposed no new taxes on corporations since the railroad tax revolt of the 1880s. Between 1900 and 1908, the state's expenditures grew twice as fast as its population.[16] The old property tax system began to show its age in alarming ways. In 1903, for example, the comptroller twice had to borrow money from special funds to make up for general fund shortfalls.[17]

Such short-term deficits had plagued state finances across the nation since the 1870s. They originated in a structural weakness of the property tax system. The property tax system was designed to translate spending increases directly into higher taxes. Once the legislature had determined the total amount to be spent, it was supposed to compare that amount with the state tax base, which was the total amount of property in the state. The ratio of expenditures to tax base would then become the tax rate.

That was how it was supposed to work. In practice, legislatures often fudged on the tax rate to make themselves more popular and get reelected. When legislators surrendered to the powerful political incentive to set the tax rate lower than they should have, they occasionally caused "embarrassment" to the state treasury by draining it completely. As long as state spending continued to grow slowly, the comptroller could continue to cover such shortfalls by borrowing from special funds, while the succeeding legislature paid for the preceding one's sins. When state spending leaped suddenly, however, because a state took on a new program—as California did in 1903 with its new commitment to free high schools—such informal procedures became increasingly difficult.

In short, spending drove taxation. In the best circumstances, the property tax system meant that higher spending led directly to higher taxes. When that system failed, usually under the stress of nonincremental spending increases, states had to adopt more robust methods of extracting resources from their citizens. State finances were the most important factor in California's movement toward taxation of corporations.

The Golden State also was powerfully influenced by the tax reform theories of the NTA. In California, the ideas of the NTA were promoted by Carl Copping Plehn, a professor at the University of California, Berkeley. Plehn was the West Coast version of E. R. A. Seligman. Like Seligman, Plehn earned his doctorate in economics in Germany and returned to the United States on fire with reform. Plehn and Seligman both belonged to the American Economic Association (AEA), which Seligman had helped found in 1885.

Plehn launched his attack on California's property tax system in 1897.[18] For the next fourteen years, he worked to replace the property tax with a system of taxation that was based on ability to pay and separation of state and local revenues. Plehn served on the state tax commission of 1906, which designed a new system of state finance that was based on the corporation tax, and toured the state building support for the idea among the state's financial and utility leaders. When the system failed to achieve adoption in the general election of 1908, Plehn advised the legislature on how to amend it and helped campaign for its ultimate passage in 1910.[19] The California plan of corporation taxation adopted in 1910 was so much the work of this one man that veteran newsmen on the Sacramento political beat called it "the Plehn Plan."[20]

In many ways, the Plehn plan for separation of revenue looked like the business-friendly state corporation taxes adopted by eastern states in the 1880s, which had allowed railroads to accept a light state tax on gross receipts in exchange for a much heavier local tax on property. As Plehn noted in his report for the 1906 tax commission, the railroads were "strongly in favor of the gross earnings tax" because of "its simplicity, the ease of administration," and its uniformity.[21] According to the Plehn plan, utilities would be taxed on their gross earnings "in lieu of all other taxes and licenses, state, county, and local, *on operative property.*"[22] Localities would still be able to assess other kinds of property, such as real estate that was owned by railroad companies but was not being used for railroad operations, but the most valuable property of the utilities would be removed from the local tax base.

City officials understood immediately why the corporations favored the state tax. When the Commonwealth Club, an organization of San Francisco's Progressive businessmen, debated the issue in 1908, its city finance section reported against the state commission's tax reform amendment. As the city finance section pointed out, corporations already were bearing the cost of municipal progress by means of their property assessments. City growth had to be funded with bonds, and every bond issue carried its own burden on property tax. As long as corporations paid the local property tax, they would be paying their fair share. "Every corporation," remarked the chairman of the city finance section, "would like to withdraw its property" from the city tax base and get into "a class by itself with a more or less fixed rate." A San Francisco municipal official showed that all three of the largest corporations in his jurisdiction would contribute less to the city under the new plan.[23] When the tax reform amendment lost in the election of 1908, the state controller ascribed its defeat to the objections of urban taxpayers, whose own property taxes would have gone up because of the removal of corporation property from the municipal tax base.[24]

In 1909, Plehn and his confederates rewrote the measure for the state legislature, this time paying attention to the demands of urban legislators. The new corporation tax amendment gave municipalities a grace period during which they could still tax corporate property for bonded debts. The state also promised to make transfer payments to compensate for lost property tax revenue. Under the new law, urban taxpayers would pay less than they had before. San Francisco taxpayers, for example, would see their total tax bill shrink by $790,000 during the first year under the new amendment. Any taxes levied by municipalities on corporate property for bond purposes would be deducted from the state's share of the corporation tax.[25]

Voters approved the amendment in 1910. It established a tax of 1 percent on the capital stock of banks and 4 percent on the gross receipts of utilities such as railroads and power companies.[26] Other corporations—such as water, oil, mining, and manufacturing firms—were taxed on their "franchises," which were defined as the par value of their corporate stock less their tangible property. As in Massachusetts, real estate, buildings, and equipment owned by such corporations remained subject to local taxation.[27]

Unlike most other state corporation taxes, the California amendment explicitly prohibited future state property taxes. Most other states left that part of the compromise as an informal agreement. The California tax amendment turned a fiscal goal into a constitutional mandate. It locked state revenues to the flat tax rate on corporate incomes. Without the option of imposing a state property tax, state officials discovered that the corporation tax would become a stumbling block instead of a stepping stone to expansion of public services.

In political terms, the measure had the support of utility and financial interests. Merchants and manufacturers, on the other hand, who were less powerful in California state politics, actually preferred local tax assessment.[28] The political logic was simple: Merchants and manufacturers depended on their hometown political clout to keep their assessments low. By the same token, utilities and banks often found their far-flung property unfairly marked up by local assessors who had nothing to fear from some distant company head-quarters.[29] Farmers and landlords, of course, supported income taxation because they expected it to take some of the tax burden off their own backs.

Wisconsin's adoption of the income tax a year later resulted from a similar combination of circumstances. Wisconsin, like California, had a mixed economy. Transportation and financial interests were well connected politically, but manufacturers and merchants were relatively weak. Like California, Wisconsin had been spending more and more on education between 1905 and 1915, although it experienced nothing like the state-level fiscal crises California suffered.[30] Finally, Wisconsin tax policy also was shaped by a prominent NTA economist: Thomas S. Adams.

Adams, an economics professor at the University of Wisconsin, was one of the NTA's leading experts on income taxation.[31] Unlike Plehn and Seligman, Adams believed that a state income tax could succeed. Seligman favored income taxation in theory but thought that an income tax could be administered only by the federal government. Adams turned out to be correct.

In 1911, a year after California enacted its corporation tax amendment, Wisconsin imposed the nation's first twentieth-century income tax. Although income taxes later became significant methods of tapping individual incomes, corporations rather than individuals carried the burden of early income taxes like Wisconsin's. Although the Wisconsin income tax allowed generous personal exemptions, it granted almost none to corporations. During the first year of its operation, when it was expected to bring in about $1 million in revenue, the Wisconsin income tax generated about $3.5 million. Corporations paid $2 million of that amount.[32] The Wisconsin income tax imposed slightly higher rates on corporations than existing corporation taxes such as California's. Whereas California levied a flat 1 or 4 percent, depending on the type of corporation, the Wisconsin income tax imposed a progressive tax rate ranging from 2 to 6 percent, depending on earnings.[33]

Because railroads and utilities already were paying relatively high taxes on the basis of the 1903 *ad valorem* reassessment law, they were exempt from the Wisconsin income tax and therefore did not oppose it in the legislature. As in California, manufacturing firms, which would be hardest hit by the income tax, lacked enough political clout to put a stop to the new tax measure.[34] Utilities and banks did not actively seek out income taxation or conspire to put one over on merchants, manufacturers, and ordinary property taxpayers. The new system simply hurt banks and utilities less than it hurt manufacturers.

State officials and economists around the country paid close attention to

Wisconsin's income tax experiment. Most of them ascribed its success to its centralized system of assessment. Local assessors played no role in levying the Wisconsin income tax. Instead, the law divided the state into assessment districts that were larger than counties and assigned each one an expert assessor, who was hired through a civil service examination.[35] Several states imitated Wisconsin almost immediately. In 1912, for example, Mississippi levied a tax of 0.5 percent on individual incomes that was later applied to corporations, and in 1915 Connecticut imposed a 2 percent tax on corporate incomes.[36]

The success of Adams' idea for state income taxation in Wisconsin converted NTA godfather Seligman to the cause. In 1915, Seligman publicly recanted his previous opposition to the state income tax and recommended that his own home state follow suit. New York had to do something, Seligman concluded, to meet "the need . . . for a vastly increased revenue" created by the state's sudden frenzy of transportation spending.[37] Seligman's speech underscored the difference between the origins of income taxation in New York and Wisconsin. Wisconsin's income tax movement grew out of a combination of reform theory, rising expenditures, and political self-defense among banks and utilities. In New York, fiscal necessity was the mother of invention. The state simply could not pay its bills without a major overhaul of its extractive capabilities. Even more clearly than in California, nonincremental spending growth drove tax reform in New York.

In 1902, with the guidance of Seligman, the patron saint of tax reform, the government of New York state attained the nirvana of complete separation of revenues. The Empire State's battery of indirect taxes—including the general corporation tax, the bank tax, and others—finally succeeded in generating enough revenue to allow the state to discontinue its property tax. From 1902 to 1910, the state collected no taxes on property.

Then, just at the moment of fiscal apotheosis, legislators and voters wrecked it all by embarking on the state's greatest transportation construction spree since the construction of the Erie Canal.[38] In addition to the canal and highway bonds of 1903 and 1905, which would not come due for years, the state's commitments to education and hospital expenditure continued to grow. The activist state was expensive, and the legislature had to find a way to pay for it. As governor John A. Dix put it, "The modern State stands for a wider conception of public duty. . . . [I]ncreasing cost of government necessitates increased revenues."[39] In 1911, the state reimposed property taxation.

The succeeding administration allowed the property tax to lapse, however, and in 1915 the state plunged into another fiscal crisis. By this time, the state property tax had become a major issue in New York politics. The incoming Republican administration claimed that the fiscal irresponsibility of the outgoing Democratic regime had forced the state to resort to a new property tax.[40] Not only had the Democratic administration of governor Martin Glynn deferred maintenance at state institutions; the legislature (a Democratic Senate and Republican Assembly) also had failed to levy a property tax when it should have done so. The 1916 New York commission on taxation agreed with Governor Dix's conclusion five years before, pointing out that "many new functions have been assumed by the State government under a policy demanded by the people," and unless there was a radical change in popular sentiment, the commission found "little likelihood" that the scope or cost of public services would shrink anytime soon, "no matter what administrative economies may be effected."[41] The commission recommended a state income tax to solve the problem.

In 1917 New York followed in the steps of Wisconsin and imposed a new income tax of 3 percent. In 1919 the state raised the rate to 4.5 percent.[42] New York's 1917 income tax, like California's 1910 corporation tax, was driven by the need for more state revenue. Nonincremental spending growth was the source of that need.

California, Wisconsin, and New York each adopted one form or another of the income tax as a result of a combination of energetic tax reform agitation and rising state expenditures. In California and Wisconsin, the political strength of utilities and banks relative to that of merchants and manufacturers facilitated the passage of income taxation. In New York, merchants and manufacturers supported the income tax. The Associated Manufacturers and Merchants of New York State, for example, reported in favor of the income tax. Although they were not happy about having to contribute more to the support of the state government, they hoped to enjoy "future security in a well regulated and administered taxation system" because "there is no security under the present chaotic condition of the tax laws of the State of New York."[43] As in Wisconsin and California, New York's business and banking interests did not conspire to impose income taxation on the state. Instead, they opted to accept a compromise that carried some costs but also offered them some benefits.

Unlike California, Wisconsin, and New York, Kansas did not adopt an income tax or a corporation tax before 1929. Although the Sunflower State had its own NTA apostle spreading the gospel of tax reform, it never suffered a fiscal crisis on the order of New York or California. In fact, its expenditures never approached even those of Wisconsin. Although several governors advocated income taxation, or at least some sort of business taxation, the legislature clung resolutely to the old property tax. The absence of high spending or a fiscal crisis in Kansas underscores the importance of state spending as a cause of the rise of the corporate state elsewhere.

Although Kansas never adopted an income or corporation tax, it did reform its state tax system in 1907 by creating a state tax commission. That reform was undertaken with the guidance of Samuel T. Howe, tax reform prophet of the Great Plains. Howe had argued for a state tax commission as early as the 1880s, when he had been state treasurer.[44] An active member of the NTA, Howe was elected president of that body in 1915.[45] He chaired the Kansas State Tax Commission from its creation in 1907 until he died in 1922.[46]

Under Howe's guidance, the tax commission made several recommendations for reform, all in line with accepted NTA principles. In 1914, for example, the commission recommended that the state constitution be amended to allow the property of corporations to be assessed on a different basis from that of individuals. The amendment failed. In 1920, the commission recommended that the state adopt a corporation franchise tax and general income tax. That amendment also failed. Finally, in 1924, voters approved the amendment originally proposed in 1914, so that corporate property and debts could be taxed differently from other property.[47]

As Howe told the story, the classification measure failed in 1914 because "the interests—you have heard that term used—got out some circulars and scattered them broadcast over the state, influencing enough votes to defeat the amendment. We had no funds to make a campaign with and so we made none." The law would have allowed the tax commission to exempt from taxation seed corn and other agricultural tools while imposing a new tax on "mineral products."[48] In fact, the law was aimed at the oil drilling companies that were springing up across Kansas as the demand for petroleum accelerated in step with the production of automobiles. Other Kansas tax officials, however, disagreed with Howe that "the interests" were the main stumbling block to reform. As one of them noted, "Our common people would probably claim that this is a socialistic scheme of some kind that would deprive them of their earnings and fruits of their work."[49] When the classification measure finally passed in1924, its most significant effect was to impose a heavier tax on mortgages and shares of bank stock rather than on oil companies.[50]

Between oil company "interests" on one hand and voters suspicious of "socialistic schemes" on the other, political conditions in Kansas proved hostile to income and corporation taxation, despite Howe's most enthusiastic efforts. The case of Kansas showed that in the absence of political support and fiscal crisis, NTA advocacy alone was insufficient to bring corporation taxes to a Jeffersonian republic.

Other Jeffersonian republics were less reluctant, but the taxes they imposed contributed only a small share of the state's total revenue. In 1917 Missouri imposed a tax of 1.5 percent on personal and corporate incomes. Massachusetts, North Dakota, and Montana all imposed income taxes in 1919.[51] By 1929 all but a handful of states imposed some sort of tax on the basis of corporate income.[52] Most of those states, however, collected such fees as license taxes and charged only nominal rates.

Before the Great Depression of the 1930s, in fact, income taxes contributed only a small share to total receipts in any state (Table 3). Only New York, Wisconsin, and Massachusetts depended on income tax revenues to any significant degree, even as late as 1929. In Mississippi, North Dakota, and Oregon—the only other states from this sample to impose income taxation before the Great Depression—the income tax was a relatively insignificant source of revenue. In the nation as a whole, income taxes accounted for only about 2 percent of state and local revenues.[53]

On the other hand, taxes on corporate incomes, which were classified separately from income taxes, remained an important source of revenue for corporate states well into the 1920s.[54] From 1910 through 1929, New York and Massachusetts consistently derived 20–30 percent of their annual receipts from corporation taxes. Pennsylvania and New Jersey collected at least 10 percent of their annual receipts from the same source. Thanks to its 1910 tax measure, California derived almost half of its annual receipts from corporation taxes. In the Jeffersonian republics of the Great Plains and Far West, corporation taxes contributed barely 5 percent of annual receipts.[55]

In New York and California, transportation expenditures played an important role in corporation tax reform because of their unique size and timing. Few other states spent so much so soon. California and New York financed their highway construction by issuing bonds that had to be paid for out of property tax receipts. Their transportation expenditures therefore became part of the existing tax structure, placing enormous strain on fiscal systems that were designed for much smaller loads. As a result, New York and California became pioneers in corporation and income taxation.

Most other states waited until 1919, when three western states invented a new form of taxation that transferred the tremendous costs of highway con-

TABLE 3. Income Tax Receipts as a Percentage
of Total State Receipts, Peak Years

State	Percentage of Total Annual Receipts	Peak Year(s)
Eastern states		
Massachusetts	20	1929
Pennsylvania	—	—
New Jersey	—	—
New York	15	1929
Southern states		
Alabama	—	—
Mississippi	7	1927
Tennessee	—	—
Midwestern states		
Wisconsin	15	1927
Illinois	—	—
Michigan	—	—
Great Plains states		
Kansas	—	—
Nebraska	—	—
North Dakota	1	1924–29
South Dakota	—	—
Far Western states		
California	—	—
Oregon	3	1926
Nevada	—	—

SOURCES: New York, Massachusetts, New Jersey, California,
Oregon, Nevada, and Wisconsin annual reports of the state
auditor and comptroller; Richard E. Sylla, John B. Legler, and
John Wallis, *Sources and Uses of Funds in State and Local
Governments, 1790–1915* [machine-readable dataset] (Ann
Arbor, Mich.: Inter-University Consortium for Political and
Social Research, 1995); and U.S. Census, *Financial Statistics
of States* (Washington, D.C.: GPO), for years after 1915.
NOTE: Dashes indicate that the state derived less than 1
percent of its total annual receipts from income taxes.

struction from the states' existing fiscal systems directly to highway users.
Where New York and California had issued highway construction bonds
backed by the states' ability to tax their citizens, Oregon, New Mexico, and
Colorado supported their highway bonds with a tax levied only on highway
users in the form of a motor vehicle fuel tax.[56] Gasoline taxes were a long-term
solution, implemented to pay for loans that those small western and southern
states would have been unable to afford otherwise. For the Jeffersonian republics, as one Tennessee tax official put it, the gasoline tax was "the giant of
history."[57]

As a revenue mechanism, the gas tax was phenomenally successful. Whereas
corporation taxes had imposed taxes ranging from 1 percent to 6 percent of

TABLE 4. Gasoline Tax Receipts as a Percentage of
Total State Receipts, Peak Years

State	Percentage of Total Annual Receipts	Peak Year(s)
Eastern states		
Massachusetts	5	1929
Pennsylvania	10	1929
New Jersey	7	1929
New York	—	—
Southern states		
Alabama	5	1929
Mississippi	8	1928
Tennessee	11	1928
Midwestern states		
Wisconsin	11	1928
Illinois	3	1928
Michigan	9	1929
Great Plains states		
Kansas	9	1928
Nebraska	19	1928
North Dakota	2	1928–29
South Dakota	10	1929
Far Western states		
California	13	1925
Oregon	10	1926
Nevada	7	1925

SOURCES: New York, Massachusetts, New Jersey, California,
Oregon, Nevada, and Wisconsin annual reports of state auditor
and comptroller; Richard E. Sylla, John B. Legler, and John
Wallis, *Sources and Uses of Funds in State and Local
Governments, 1790–1915* [machine-readable dataset] (Ann
Arbor, Mich.: Inter-University Consortium for Political and
Social Research, 1995); and U.S. Census, *Financial Statistics
of States* (Washington, D.C.: GPO), for years after 1915.
NOTE: Dashes indicate that the state derived less than 1
percent of its total annual receipts from gasoline taxes.

gross receipts, the gasoline tax imposed a levy of 25–33 percent of the retail value of the product.[58] Although that rate seems astronomical compared with corporation taxes of the time, voters hardly noticed it because the real price of gas actually declined over the course of the 1920s, and gas taxes could be tacked on without seeming to affect the price of a gallon at the pump.[59] Voters also liked the tax's obvious equity in the way it distributed the tax burdens of highway construction.[60]

Gas taxes were more important to the Jeffersonian republics than to other states (Table 4). The gas tax amounted to only 5 percent of Massachusetts' receipts, and New York did not enact a gas tax before the Great Depression. In contrast, Nebraska, one of the most die-hard small-government states, brought in 19 percent of its total receipts in 1928 by means of the gasoline tax. The gas tax accounted for 11 percent of Tennessee's receipts in 1928, 10 percent of South Dakota's in 1929, and 10 percent of Oregon's in 1926.

The gasoline tax helped the Jeffersonian republics fund transportation expenditures without increasing their demands on other sources of revenue. Without the need to crank up other forms of taxation to pay for highway construction, the gas tax allowed states such as Nebraska to keep building roads without upsetting the old order of property taxation. In that way, the gas tax may even have helped prevent the adoption of income taxes or other sorts of taxation in smaller states in the South and Great Plains.

Between 1910 and 1929, the most progressive states shifted their fiscal systems to solid dependence on corporate wealth. Rising expenditures for public services caused periodic fiscal crises under the old property tax system. Popular but expensive measures such as free textbooks and high schools, as well as hospital renovations and teacher salary raises after World War I, underlay an even more popular and expensive highway construction campaign. Not only did progressive states have to keep paying the bills for their old services; they had to scramble to figure out how to pay for the new ones as well. Nonincremental spending growth forced states such as New York and California to find new sources of revenue. California instituted a drastic corporation tax in 1910; Wisconsin resorted to the income tax in 1911, with New York and Massachusetts following in 1917 and 1919, respectively. Those states made corporations pay the price of progress by means of a battery of taxes on corporations, banks, utilities, and, ultimately, incomes.

By 1929, New York and Massachusetts drew more than one-third of their gross annual receipts from the corporation tax and the income tax. To a lesser extent, California, New Jersey, and Pennsylvania also relied on taxes levied on corporate capital or incomes. While state officials congratulated themselves on having solved the great fiscal problem of their time, their new partners outside the government already were making plans for improving the way their tax dollars were being spent.

SEVEN

The Test of Democracy

CONTROLLING SPENDING IN THE CORPORATE STATE,
1907 TO 1929

In 1906, a year before E. R. A. Seligman helped found the National Tax Association, he was already well known as a tax expert, not only for his academic publications but for his work on the 1899 Ford franchise tax bill. In addition to his teaching duties at Columbia University, Seligman was serving on the New York City mayor's Advisory Commission on Taxation and Finance—popularly known as the McClellan Commission. One of Seligman's colleagues on the commission, Frederick A. Cleveland, got Seligman interested in a project he was working on. Cleveland, a lawyer with a doctorate in economics, was teaching finance at New York University and was working for the public accounting firm of Haskins and Sells. Cleveland had several major backers already lined up for his special project, including the New York City Citizens' Union and the New York City Chamber of Commerce. Cleveland's project involved gathering a group of finance and management experts to help the New York City government adopt the best practices of business management. Intrigued, Seligman agreed to serve as the first chairman of the board of directors of the New York Bureau of Municipal Research (NYBMR).[1]

Over the next quarter-century, the NYBMR became a model for a new kind of nonprofit organization. Whether they were called municipal research bureaus, government research bureaus, or taxpayers' associations, their mission was the same: They wanted to maximize government efficiency; they wanted to get the biggest bang for the taxpayers' buck. In the language of the day, they wanted to bring business methods to government. Between 1906 and 1929, government research bureaus spread across the nation, investigating, reporting, and making recommendations. Their trademark product was the "survey," a genre of fact-finding report of which the most famous example was Crystal Eastman's *Pittsburgh Survey* of 1908. Government research bureaus were the prototypes of the efficiency consultants that came to be known later in the twentieth century as think tanks.

Government research bureaus were one side effect of the exponential growth of government services and taxation that characterized the corporate state. Corporation and income taxes had several unintended consequences that grew out of one simple proposition: If business had to pay for progress, government would have to get more businesslike. Corporation taxes brought business officials into government in new roles, formal and informal. Corporation taxes contributed indirectly to the rise of government research bureaus, which in turn directed a wave of state government reorganizations throughout the 1910s. The most strident taxpayers' associations joined the United States Chamber of Commerce in publishing propaganda that often shaded into outright electioneering.

The new relationship between business and government, particularly in states where corporation and income taxes supplied a significant share of revenues, completed their transformation into corporate states. In contrast, states that relied less on corporation and income taxes maintained a more distant relationship with business. The different roles of business officials showed the most obvious distinction in each state's tax administration between the corporate states and the Jeffersonian republics. In California and New York, for example, business officials found informal advisory positions in tax administration. In Kansas, on the other hand, business officials did not participate in the state's tax machinery.

In California, New York, and Kansas, tax administration involved two groups of officials: the state tax commission (in some cases called the board of equalization) and county assessors. The state tax commission was responsible for assessing property that was subject to the state corporation tax, such as railroad cars and tracks, telephone and telegraph wires and poles, and pipelines. It also calculated gross and net earnings and rates of return for corporation income taxes. Even in Kansas, the state tax commission assessed the property of utility companies operating in more than one county, then divided up the total value among the various counties, depending on the proportion located in each one. The state tax commissions also were responsible for equalizing the real estate assessments reported by each county, raising or lowering assessments as necessary. The state tax commission's everyday work was done mostly in the office. Corporations delivered the documents necessary to prove their worth or income; the state tax commission then determined a value and charged a tax bill. Before 1910, state tax commissions usually consisted of three to five commissioners and a small office staff. As state corporation taxes grew increasingly complex and comprehensive, state tax commissions began to expand, hiring engineers and other experts to investigate and verify the corporations' returns.[2]

The other main group of officials who administered state taxes were county assessors. County assessors were responsible for assessing all property that was subject to local taxation. Even in New York and California, they assessed for local taxation all corporate real estate, buildings, and equipment that was not covered by the state corporation tax, which amounted to a significant share of many local tax bases. In Kansas they assessed all corporate property except property that belonged to utilities running through more than one county. They also were responsible for assessing all other real estate and personal property. Some of their work could be done in the office, by recopying tax rolls of previous years. Much of their work had to be done in the field, however, through on-site inspections of various kinds of property. In most cases they were the main point of contact between government and the taxpayer. As one New York official put it in 1924, "We are the long hand of the government that reaches into the banker's wallet, the farmer's jeans, the laborer's overalls, and the clerk's pay envelope to extract the government's tithe."[3]

County assessors in New York, California, and Kansas met annually to discuss the issues of their work. In California and New York, assessors met on a voluntary basis; in Kansas the meeting was a legal requirement. California county assessors formed a voluntary association in 1902, with subsequent annual meetings. Despite their requests that the state make the meetings mandatory and subsidize their travel, the association remained voluntary through 1929.[4] In New York, county assessors began to meet voluntarily in 1916 in conjunction with the annual state tax conference.[5] The tax reform legislation that established the Kansas State Tax Commission 1907 gave that body formal power of supervision over county assessors. The commission therefore was required by law to call all county assessors together every two years to go over assessment procedures and compare notes.[6] Those meetings revealed the everyday business of each state's tax system as seen through the eyes of officials on the front lines.

County tax assessors in all three states seemed to take genuine pride in their work. Their annual meetings often took on the tone of fraternal society gatherings, with members referring to each other as "brother assessors." Well aware of their public reputation as "the main 'fall guy' of the county, sometimes designated as the assessor, more often designated as that ———," they indulged occasionally in gallows humor.[7] The following poem, written by a tax official in Michigan, was read at the 1926 meeting of the Kansas assessors. It is worth quoting in full not only for its content, which offers a vivid impression of the everyday work of rural property tax assessors, but also for what its reading implies about the annual meetings of Kansas county assessors.

Taking the Assessment

When Coolidge took his office and commenced to draw his pay,
The papers said that confidence had settled down to stay;
When the flowers commenced to blossom and bees began to hum,
We went out assessing farmers—prosperity had come.

Our instructions were to hustle and ferret out the facts;
We must find out all the farmer had and then daub on the tax;
We must tax him for his horses, his cattle, sheep and hog,
And last of all, but not the least, a dollar for his dog.

We did not find the farmers rolling round in wealth,
But found the mud a-plenty for comfort or for health;
The great wave of prosperity had settled down, no doubt;
Had settled thick upon the rich, but left the farmer out.

The farmers seemed quite willing their share of tax to pay,
And told us all their neighbors had, in quite a friendly way;
We marked down all their cattle and counted up the hogs;
'Twas strange how many farmers had just got out of dogs.

We visited a lady's house—her name I can't recall;
She came from where the breezes blow, way down at Montreal;
She told me in broken French, but with a charming grace,
They didn't, hadn't got no dog round there on the place.

A neighbor had just posted me on next adjoining farm;
So I went out upon a scout around the lady's barn;
A prop stood up against the door—I knew just what it meant—
To kick that prop and find a dog would be a great event.

I kicked the prop, the door flew wide—great heavens there were two
The moment that I saw their teeth I knew just what to do;
I started for the barnyard fence, and got there mighty quick;
I heard the dogs a-coming, and the woman hollowed "Sic."

They filled their mouths with clothing and stopped to chew the goods;
I shingled myself with assessment roll and sauntered to the woods;
I tried to patch my clothing with strips of elm bark;
I stayed around the woods all day and come home after dark.

This taught me quite a lesson in visiting other farms—
I never tried to meddle with the props around the barns;
In all of my experience this was the nearest call—
The lady that didn't got no dog, and came from Montreal.[8]

Aside from what this bit of doggerel says about the ability of county assessors not to take themselves too seriously, it provides colorful images of the work of rural county assessors. It also is an important reminder that even in 1926, the agrarian world of the Jeffersonian republic persisted alongside the corporate state.

In addition to assessing farmers, rural county assessors in states such as Kansas dealt with corporate officials as well. In Kansas, the two main types of firms assessed by local officials were banks and oil companies. In its role as board of equalization, the state tax commission found itself lowering bank assessments as often as it raised them. As one Kansas assessor commented in 1922, "There are a great number of county assessors present here that pick out the bank as the one institution that ought to pay tax on actual value. . . . The bank, as compared with other institutions, is now paying its just proportion of taxes."[9]

Oil companies, on the other hand, were a mixed lot. In a general discussion about their experiences assessing Standard Oil in 1911, most of the assessors found that the petroleum giant had cooperated amiably.[10] A decade later, however, several county assessors reported serious difficulties in collecting taxes due from wildcat oil drillers. Two assessors had to confiscate drilling rigs to secure payment for back taxes. The confrontations they related to their brother assessors were epic: "I said, 'I propose to hold this stuff until the taxes are paid.' He said, 'We have dealt with a lot of people as smart as you are,' and I said, 'I have dealt with a great many crooks, perhaps crookeder than you, and you will not move that stuff out of Ellsworth county until you pay that tax.'"[11] On the other hand, other assessors had better experiences with the oil companies, especially larger firms. "I don't want the county clerks of the state of Kansas to go on record as against the oil companies," protested a colleague of the fearless assessor from Ellsworth County. "I agree with the gentleman over yonder that some small oil companies are little and mean, but you take the Sinclair and the Prairie Oil and Gas, and I find that they are very liberal. They give us good assessments."[12] The Kansas county assessors dealt with the good, the bad, and the ugly corporations. The practical application of the old property tax to corporation property was sometimes confrontational, sometimes cooperative.

Unlike their fellow public servants in Kansas, the county assessors of New York and California invited outsiders to their annual gatherings. In many cases those outsiders were representatives of the very banks and oil companies that the Kansas assessors stared down. Significantly, those guest speakers often addressed the topic of state expenditures. In California, for example, just two years after the 1910 passage of the corporation tax act, tax agents from a dozen firms—including utilities, steam railroads, and street railways—attended the annual meeting of the County Assessors' Association.[13] In an address to the assembled corporate officials and county assessors, J. F. Sartori, president of the Security Trust and Savings Bank of Los Angeles, warned that the recently passed school textbook amendment would raise state spending beyond what the current corporation tax rate could support. He recommended special taxes on automobiles and liquor dealers and reimposition of the poll tax. As a last resort, he concluded reluctantly, he supposed the state might raise corporation tax rates—"if it is found justifiable."[14]

Nor did the California county supervisors shy away from political issues of the day, especially when they touched on a subject as close to home as taxation. In 1920, for example, the president of the association noted that the "single tax proponents" had put an "unwise and disastrous" initiative on the ballot to replace the state's corporation tax system with a single tax on the growth of real estate values. "We must use whatever influence we have," urged the president, "singly or as a body, to encompass its downfall." The group voted unanimously to "use their influence for its defeat at the polls."[15]

The state-level counterpart of the county assessors, the state board of equal-

ization, seemed equally impressed with the advice of its new corporate partners. For example, in its annual report of 1914 the board suggested that railroad regulation could hurt state revenues because any rate reductions by the
railroad commission would reduce taxable incomes. Railroads therefore should
get to pay lower corporation taxes or charge higher rates. With regard to utilities, the board went on, the trend toward municipal ownership also could cut
into state finances by removing valuable firms from the state's tax base. Even
the insurance industry got a plug, as the board of equalization pointed out that
the new state industrial accident board would be taking away taxable premium
revenue from private accident insurance companies.[16] In the annual meetings
of California county assessors, corporation officials were important opinion
makers, working in the very heart of the state's taxation machinery to advance
their own causes. Lower school spending, reduced railroad regulation, opposition to municipal ownership of utilities and the single tax were advocated by
corporation officials and taken up by county assessors and the state board of
equalization.

The attorney's impression was accurate. "Well, I have been a corporation
Although New York's county assessors also invited corporation representatives to their annual meetings, neither the assessors nor the state tax commission seemed to be as impressed by their private-sector advisors as their California colleagues had been. In 1916, for example, at the first annual meeting
of the county assessors, the tax attorney of Western Union Telegraph Company complained at length about the irregular local assessments his firm received from various school districts throughout the state. In New York, the
physical property of all utilities was taxable by the localities; the state taxed
only the gross earnings and capital stock of transmission companies.[17] As a result, Western Union's local taxes added up to a significant sum. The attorney's
main complaint, however, was not the size of the payment but the method. He
objected to the fact that there was no statewide, standardized date for local
tax assessments. "There is not a day in my office," he fumed, "that I do not
get a New York tax bill!" Not that he expected satisfaction from the tax commission, however, because "the present State Tax Commission has very little
regard for corporations."[18]

The attorney's impression was accurate. "Well, I have been a corporation
tax attorney for a good many years," retorted the president of the state tax
commission. "That is where I learned the business." He suggested that unpredictable billing was no worse than many corporate tax dodges he had seen,
such as locating a bogus corporate headquarters building in a distant county
to avoid high local taxes.[19] In fact, 1916 was the year that the New York tax

commission reorganized itself into three new divisions specializing in water, gas, and electric; telephone and telegraph; and steam railroads. The newly hired experts discovered millions of dollars in property value by reexamining old assessments.

In New York, then, introduction of corporate officials into the state tax machinery seemed to have just the opposite effect it had in California. Whereas corporation officials pushed California toward more lenient treatment of corporations, just the reverse was true in New York. By suborning a corporation lawyer to serve as president of the state tax commission, New York tax administrators scored a major coup in their ongoing struggle to make the corporations pay their fair share. Indeed, corporation officials in New York seemed to have a more difficult time with the state than they had in Kansas. Nevertheless, the exchange of personnel between the private and public sectors and the presence of corporation lawyers arguing their cause in front of the county assessors' meeting marked important differences between tax administration in New York and Kansas.

Another difference between California and New York was the informal role of corporate officials in the state legislature. That difference sprang from the particular mechanisms of the two states' taxes. New York imposed on corporations a complicated mix of taxes on property, capital stock, and earnings. In contrast, California imposed a more-or-less flat income tax, leaving only the rate to be determined by the legislature. In California, that approach made the corporation tax rate a political issue of utmost importance to the businesses in question.

Business lobbyists, of course, had been no strangers to the statehouses of America in the nineteenth century. In 1883, for example, publication of the Huntington-Colton letters showed the power exercised by the Southern Pacific Railroad over the California legislature.[20] Likewise, New York's 1905 Armstrong investigation revealed the insurance industry's machinations in the government of the Empire State.[21] Once corporation tax rates became subject to legislative fiat, however, corporations took an even more intense interest in what went on in the state capitol.

In California, the "new lobby," as one veteran newspaperman remarked, was a different breed from the old Southern Pacific manipulators. Professionals and experts from the various industries that were subject to the new state tax came to tell legislators exactly how much their enterprises should contribute to the expenses of the state. Many of the new lobbyists were former state employees who had sold their administrative expertise to the highest corporate bidder. Others were "high-salaried attorneys, experts in finance, engineering and taxation." Any one of them might receive fees equal to the payroll of the entire Senate and Assembly for the session.[22]

In 1913 and 1915, California legislators got their first taste of what it would be like to raise the corporation tax rate under the new order. In both sessions, legislators achieved only token success.[23] The 1915 rate hike was so small that the state had to reimpose a corporate license tax, which it had abolished in 1913.[24] The real confrontation between the legislature and the new lobby, however, came in 1921, when the legislature proposed to change the method of calculating taxable corporate revenue. The state needed more revenue to pay for the teacher salary raise approved by popular vote the previous year.[25] In response, banks, insurance companies, and utilities sent a team of advocates to Sacramento who were so well paid they became known as the "billion dollar lobby."[26] They even brought the architect of California's entire corporation tax system, Carl Plehn himself, to argue against the reassessment bill.[27] After a massive newspaper campaign against the bill, in which its foes claimed that the state needed so much money only because of waste and extravagance in administration, the measure finally passed.[28] The outcome of the 1921 reassessment fight brought back ghosts of the railroad tax revolt of the 1880s. In both cases, corporations fought the tax in court for years. Several firms managed to put off paying their taxes under the 1921 reassessment law until 1926, when the U.S. Supreme Court finally decided in favor of the state.[29]

New roles in state government for corporation officials distinguished corporate states such as California and New York from Jeffersonian republics such as Kansas, where business and government stayed more firmly at arms' length. Those new roles resulted directly from corporation tax reforms. Corporation tax reform also had a significant indirect effect in corporate states. That effect contributed to the rise of government research bureaus such as the NYBMR.

The relationship between rising taxes and the foundation of the NYBMR was not one of simple cause and effect. According to NYBMR leaders, it was more a case of using tax reform sentiment to achieve their own ends. In 1924, for example, when NYBMR director Luther Gulick addressed the New York county assessors' meeting, he declared baldly, "The problem of economy and efficiency in government is basically a problem of harnessing these forces of tax opposition in such a way that they will bear directly upon the administration of government."[30] In his introduction to a 1966 history of the NYBMR, Gulick dismissed the idea that "the leaders of the reform were more interested in 'efficiency,' 'economy,' 'science,' 'business methods,' and 'tax reduction' than in the ends or means of effective democracy" as a "superficial appraisal."[31] Nevertheless, it seems clear that many of the NYBMR's earliest supporters had financial motivations. J. P. Morgan; Kuhn, Loeb, & Co.; and Henry Morgenthau, for example, had an immediate material interest in the management of city financial affairs because their firms bought most of New York's municipal bond issues during the period. How the city was run had a direct effect on the value of their investments.[32]

If the connections between corporation taxes and the origins of the NYBMR were ambiguous, however, that was not the case with another class of governmental research bureaus: taxpayers' associations. Whereas bureaus of municipal research focused on finding facts and providing disinterested advice to government administrators, taxpayers' associations focused on advocacy for tax reduction.[33] Groups such as the California Taxpayers' Association, however, were careful to position themselves within the reform tradition of the governmental research bureau movement.[34]

Business methods were the holy grail of the government research bureaus. "If there is one field of human achievement in which American ingenuity has gained recognition," Gulick explained to the New York tax assessors, "it is in the administration of business undertakings. . . . There is hardly a problem of public administration which cannot be solved through the application of ideas developed by American business enterprises."[35] Like the word "progressive," the phrase "business methods" was used so often to describe so many different things that it became almost meaningless in the first decades of the twentieth century. To Gulick and other experts in the government research bureau movement, however, the phrase had a very specific meaning. It included adoption of an executive budget, centralized purchasing and accounting, and uniform personnel classification. Many of those goals were realized in the state reorganization movement that began in 1911 and lasted through the 1920s.

In 1910, president William Howard Taft announced his intention to apply those concepts to the federal government by creating the National Commission on Economy and Efficiency.[36] Several states immediately followed suit. Wisconsin created a state commission on reorganization in 1911; it was followed by New Jersey and Massachusetts in 1912 and Iowa, Illinois, Pennsylvania, New York, and Minnesota in 1913.[37] During the years between 1910 and 1925, most states created some kind of reorganization commission, and many followed through by adopting those commissions' recommendations.

The New York proposal epitomized the goals of the state reorganization movement. In 1914, the one-year-old State Department of Efficiency and Economy began to prepare a series of recommendations for the state constitutional convention planned for the following year. The NYBMR devoted extensive resources to the New York state survey. Frederick Cleveland himself, one of the bureau's founders, collaborated on the report with historian Charles Beard and a staff of twenty researchers. The most important feature of the proposed constitutional amendments was centralization of authority in the executive. The governor would become almost a prime minister, with the authority to initiate a budget, appoint department heads, advocate measures before the legislature, submit measures directly to the voters, and even dismiss the legislature entirely.[38]

The list of delegates to the convention read like a "who's who" of past and future state and national leaders. Elihu Root—former secretary of war and secretary of state, 1913 winner of the Nobel Peace Prize, and admirer of Alexander Hamilton—chaired the convention. Other delegates included Seth Low, president of Columbia University and former mayor of New York City; former secretary of war Henry L. Stimson; future governor and presidential candidate Al Smith; and future senator Robert F. Wagner.[39]

Although the convention passed many of the proposed amendments, the proposals failed in the general election of 1915, mainly because they placed too much power at the disposal of the governor. In 1918, however, when Al Smith was elected governor, he appointed a new commission that included Charles Beard and planner Robert Moses to study the problem of state reorganization. Many of the new commission's recommendations were adopted by constitutional amendment in 1925, ultimately consolidating the government into sixteen departments and installing a budget system under the authority of the governor.[40]

The executive budget was a significant innovation because it finally put an end to the old hodge-podge system of legislative appropriation. Whereas the old system had left the preparation of a spending bill up to the legislature, the new system placed that responsibility in the executive branch, as Alexander Hamilton had proposed in the *Federalist*.[41] At the top of an administrative structure that stretched down through chiefs of highway, welfare, and education departments, the governor could systematically review spending requests submitted by every institution in every department and decide on a rational spending plan.[42]

Ironically, the reorganization movement had the most significant fiscal and administrative impact not on the corporate states, with their hundreds of separate commissions going in different directions at once, but on the Jeffersonian republics, with their much smaller administrations. In Jeffersonian states such as Illinois, Nebraska, and Tennessee, reorganization swept through the government in a single legislative session or election, producing significant fiscal changes almost overnight. In Illinois, for example, a single massive statutory revision known as the Civil Administrative Code combined approximately 100 commissions into 9 departments and centralized authority over them in the office of the governor.[43] Social work pioneer and University of Chicago professor Sophonisba P. Breckinridge identified the Illinois reorganization of 1917 as the moment when the old commissions of charities and corrections were first transformed into departments of public welfare because other states copied that departmental designation in their own reorganizations.[44]

After Nebraska reorganized its state government in 1919, the governor used his new power to slash spending by $2 million in 1922. In a small Jeffersonian republic that relied almost exclusively on property taxation, that action translated immediately into a reduction of state taxes by one-third.[45] In Tennessee, the Nashville Chamber of Commerce hired an expert from the NYBMR to prepare a reorganization plan in 1921. In 1922, when the incoming governor was elected on a retrenchment platform, the legislature approved the plan. Although several department chiefs sued the governor when their jobs were eliminated by the reorganization, the state supreme court upheld the law. By 1927, the reorganization had helped Tennessee erase a $3 million deficit, accumulate a $1 million surplus, and reduce taxes by one-sixth.[46] With smaller total spending to start with, Jeffersonian republics had an easier time reducing expenditures after reorganization.

Pennsylvania was the only large corporate state that was able to duplicate the smaller Jeffersonian states' success with reorganization. In 1921 the legislature appointed a reorganization commission, which cooperated with governor Gifford Pinchot in 1923 to draft a new administrative code that the legislature approved the same year. By 1926, the code's new features, especially salary classification and standardization, had paid off a $29 million deficit in the state's operating budget.[47]

Introduction of the executive budget and reorganization of state governments into departments with centralized control over personnel and purchasing brought business methods to corporate states and Jeffersonian republics alike by the late 1920s. As with the formation of government research bureaus, reorganization of state governments was not a direct result of corporation taxes or high state expenditures. In fact, just the opposite was true. Jeffersonian republics were more likely than corporate states to be dramatically affected by

the reorganization movement. The reorganization movement did not necessarily create any new relationships between government and business or be-
stow new powers on government. Its main effect was simply to reduce expenditures in some states.

In the mid-1920s, business officials began to get involved in state government in another capacity. A general public-relations campaign spearheaded by
the United States Chamber of Commerce encouraged businessmen to take an
interest in politics.[48] Articles in various business publications urged business
leaders to reduce taxes by controlling government spending. Although business writers rarely advocated specific measures, they published numerous articles recommending against high public spending and high taxes.

State and local taxation began to attract the attention of the national business press during the mid-1920s, thanks in part to federal fiscal policy. During
the first World War, the federal government imposed a special income tax to
tap the huge windfalls that certain industries reaped from wartime profits. After the war ended, the federal government repealed the excess profits tax and
embarked on a campaign of debt reduction and retrenchment. The reduction
in federal taxation was made even more dramatic by the simultaneous explosion in state and local taxation.[49]

Four years after his unsuccessful lobbying efforts on behalf of California
corporations against the corporate tax rate hike of 1920, California tax expert
Carl Plehn published an article in *Nation's Business* arguing that "the best way
out" of high taxes "is a curtailment of public spending."[50] In 1925, the Bank
of America surveyed American state debts to find out why states were issuing
so many new bonds. Highways, of course, came first, accounting for 40 percent of all the new state debts, followed by veterans' bonuses and waterways.
According to Bank of America president Edward C. Delafield, the survey
showed how important it was for businessmen to be aware of "the trends in
State financing if large-scale governmental enterprises are to be controlled in
a scientific, businesslike manner."[51]

Two years later, the United States Chamber of Commerce turned its attention to the sudden surge in state and local taxation and expenditure. As the
National Industrial Conference Board noted, the sharp reduction in federal
taxation that year made state and local taxes seem even higher.[52] In the spring
of 1927, several business periodicals picked up the Chamber's press releases
about the rising costs of state and local government. *The Index* and *System*
magazine published articles complaining that corporation taxes amounted to
one-third of net profits across all industries. In some industries, such as min-

ing, corporation income taxes exceeded profits. Nationwide, corporations paid about two-thirds of all income taxes.[53] As *System* concluded, however, most of those expenditures went to education and transportation, which were "benefits Business wants to help spread. . . . The question, it seems to me, is rather . . . how economically are the taxes to be expended?"[54] Taxation in general, and income and corporation taxes in particular, motivated business officials to get involved in government. "Perhaps at no point," declared one editor, "are business and government more interwoven than at the point of taxation and public expenditures."[55]

In the late 1920s, state taxpayers' associations followed the lead of the bureaus of municipal reform by offering survey research and recommendations to state administrations. In 1928, for example, the California Taxpayers' Association (CTA) analyzed budget requests from the state's educational, medical, and correctional institutions. The association suggested that by "controlling" wage increases and the costs of materials and supplies, all of the institutions' requests could be reduced. The CTA shared its research with various government agencies, including the department of institutions, the budget department, and the governor, working with those agencies "in the budget hearings and outside of hearings wherever assistance could be rendered." The CTA complimented "the splendid attitude of the state officials and their willingness to consider the facts" while providing good care for inmates and "hold[ing] down charges for the taxpayer."[56] The CTA worked informally and directly with state agencies, despite its lack of a legal institutional role.

By the 1920s, state taxpayers' associations also concerned themselves with controlling the fiscal desires of the general public. Because the largest expenditures of the 1920s, especially highways, had to be financed with bonds, most of those measures had to go through popular referenda. "The people as a whole—the voters—are demanding a large part of this expenditure," declared a delegate at the 1925 meeting of the NTA. "If the business interest of the country can change the attitudes and opinions of the voters on the subject, well and good."[57] At the following year's meeting, a member of the New Mexico Taxpayers' Association announced that "the real test of democracy is going to come on this question of being able to control expenditures. . . . How are you going to get this to the people except through unofficially supported agencies like the bureaus of municipal research . . . or taxpayers' associations?"[58] The revolution in politics wrought by the spread of the referendum for municipal and state-level projects, especially for transportation infrastructure, forced taxpayers' associations to take their efficiency campaigns to the hustings.

By the eve of the Great Depression, three trends had brought business methods to state government. Two of those trends—government research bureaus and the state reorganization movement—originated in corporate states and then spread to the Jeffersonian republics. The third trend, involvement of business officials in state tax bureaucracies, was unique to corporate states, but its effect was not uniform or monolithic. Entry of business officials into state tax administration did not always lead to capture of the state by taxed industries. In New York, entry of corporation lawyers into the state bureaucracy actually improved the state's ability to assess and tax corporations. In contrast, California business representatives virtually took over the state tax administration.

Tax reformers such as Carl Plehn and E. R. A. Seligman ultimately shared the goals of the United States Chamber of Commerce: They wanted to control spending. Accretion of public services had driven taxes to the point that tax reformers and businessmen alike now sought to centralize state power to get government growth under control. Ironically, their methods for controlling spending had much in common with the trends toward centralization and state power that had jacked up state spending in the first place. Politically active businessmen—the scions of the corporate state—began to attack the very conditions that had brought them to life. More than anyone, they could appreciate that their demands to increase state power to limit state spending were Hamiltonian means to Jeffersonian ends.

Conclusion

THE PRICE OF PROGRESS

"When his local chamber of commerce first appointed a tax committee . . . [the average businessman] was taunted good-naturedly by economists and political scientists and told that he would not dare to touch schools and roads." That was the story according to Morris Edwards of the United States Chamber of Commerce, as he related it to the New York State Conference of Local Assessors in 1930. Yet those were the very areas that most needed "improved and more economical administration"; furthermore, "the pressure for reduced taxes, as a matter of plain, immediate necessity, is growing unmistakably."[1] In his thumbnail explanation of why business was interested in public administration, Edwards pointed to schools and roads, two of the "big three" programs of state and local government between 1877 and 1929. The third, of course, was mental health care. Soaring spending on those three programs drove taxes to the point at which businessmen such as Edwards felt obliged to get involved in government.

During the half-century between Reconstruction and the Great Depression, a wide variety of new government programs came into being under the Progressive umbrella. Juvenile courts, workmen's compensation, clean food and drug laws, parkland conservation, antitrust policy, civil service reform, women's suffrage, and mothers' pensions were all considered important examples of progress. All of those developments represented new public services offered by American government. They expanded government's power to give.

These developments, however, did not necessitate an equal expansion of government's power to take away. In state budgets, none of those programs—even parkland conservation—came close to the enormous cost of caring for the insane, let alone the king's ransoms needed to educate children and build highways. Even at the municipal level, the grimy physical infrastructure of pavement, sewers, and streetlights rather than glamorous crusades against sweatshops and slumlords drove cities to seek vast new taxing powers from the state legislature.

The power to take money away from the greatest industrial and financial conglomerates in the world came at a price. If business had to pay for an activist state, the activist state would have to be run like a business. In the compromise of corporation taxation, business acknowledged that only its enormous pools of capital could fund the services Americans expected from progressive state governments. In turn, those states had to accept a certain amount of involvement on the part of the corporations. Both sides had something to offer, and, in general, both sides benefited. Business needed educated workers and better transportation, and government needed better management.

The American corporate state originated in high-spending, high-taxing commonwealths such as New York, Massachusetts, and California, then spread outward in the form of the state reorganization movement to the Jeffersonian republics of the South and the Great Plains. States such as Tennessee, Illinois, and Nebraska, which had never spent much on anything and collected almost nothing in corporation taxes, adopted business methods in state reorganization movements modeled on those of their more corporate neighbors. Despite the diffusion of the reorganization movement, many states succeeded in keeping government small and resisting the incursion of business methods until well after 1929.

A mix of economic, institutional, and political causes determined the timing of each state's corporate turn. Each state's economy—whether industrial, mixed, or agricultural—set the ground rules for the sorts of firms that would dominate the political landscape. Nonpartisan reformers; activist state agencies, especially with expert staffs of doctors or engineers; and the initiative and the referendum, with their potential for breaking loose from the parsimony of partisanship, were all important institutional factors in the growth of public services. Finally, the activism of tax reformers and other interest groups affected each state's methods of taxation and administration.

In the industrial economies of the northeastern states, manufacturing tended to be protected from corporation taxes at the expense of utilities. In the mixed economies of the Midwest and the Far West, the situation was reversed because utilities wielded more political power than manufacturers. In the agrarian economies of the South and the Great Plains, the politics of business revolved around regulation rather than taxation. Neither political reformers nor business representatives seized on corporation taxes as a significant issue. Instead, business influence came to those states as an imported administrative reform.

States with frequent initiatives and referenda tended to spend and tax more, provoking corporate influence sooner. The initiative and the referendum allowed the electorate at large to bypass stingy partisan legislatures, freeing state capacity for massive debt issues. In states with debt limitations dating to the 1840s, virtually every major public service measure involving significant expenditure or taxation had to be approved as a constitutional amendment. Such a proposal automatically triggered a referendum, even if it had been introduced by the state legislature. After the advent of the initiative, a popular election also could originate from any group that was capable of mobilizing voters on the basis of their own interests.

The mechanism of the initiative and the referendum discouraged partisanship and mobilized voters on the basis of their economic self-interest.[2] "The masses of the people," remarked New York state senator Henry W. Hill, chief architect of the 1903 barge canal campaign, "do not give that consideration to referendum measures submitted under the Constitution of this State that their importance deserves." For "the people affected," however, Hill continued, "a popular campaign with such an economic proposition under consideration may be far more important . . . than a political campaign howsoever momentous."[3] The key phrase was "for the people affected." Only the people affected had an interest in voting for the referendum. Significantly, Hill used the phrase "political campaigns" to distinguish elections involving candidates from referendum elections, suggesting that the latter were not political. As most Americans understood the word around the turn of the twentieth century, "politics" meant partisanship. In an era when a voter's party affiliation was still deeply rooted in his or her ethnic and cultural identity, partisan mobilization invoked powerful personal loyalties. A nonpartisan election simply was not interesting—unless you happened to be one of the people affected.[4]

The nonpartisan, issue-oriented nature of referenda created alliances that were based on pure economic self-interest. A 1939 study of the referendum and the initiative in California concluded that those mechanisms had not empowered any general constituency that might fit the vague Progressive notion of "the people." Instead, "the existing and newly established 'special interests' have accommodated themselves to the new procedures."[5] In fact, the analysis itself led to an early formulation of the theory of pluralism. Ordinary voters, "the great mass of individuals who are not formally represented by professional organizers of pressure groups and whose interests are not championed by paid lobbyists," had no place in such a system unless they could find "some interest-group whose aims parallel those of the mass of the people."[6]

Government agencies played an important role in the growth of state capacity as well. As a New York legislative committee noted in 1926, "In many cases the movement which produces change is itself the result of governmental investigation. . . . Both the bureau of labor statistics and the department of health have contributed to developments in their respective fields. . . . In a similar manner the board of charities has unquestionably played an important role in the growth of state welfare activity during the last half century."[7]

As the committee noted in its nod to the board of charities, nonpartisan expertise was a necessary condition of the state's ability to cause its own expansion. In California, expert agencies wielded similar influence. In the 1919 highway bond issue and the 1920 teacher salary measure, for example, the state engineer and the superintendent of public instruction led publicity campaigns that helped decide the elections.

Pure spending itself was not enough to cause tax reform. The work of individuals such as David Wells, E. R. A. Seligman, Curtis Guild Jr., and Carl Plehn was essential in bringing about changes in each state's tax system. Although the ideas of the NTA had nationwide currency, determined reformers had to work to implement tax reform in each state. Even then, their success depended on the balance of political power among the state's various industries.

By 1929, the simple dichotomy between corporate states and Jeffersonian republics no longer did justice to the variety of financial and administrative schemes that proliferated among the states. In commonwealths such as New York and California, where the corporate state had originated in high spending and business reactions against taxation, two different scenarios had played out. In the first scenario, states that experienced administrative reorganization and increased corporate influence spent more than they had before. New York fit such a "corporate liberal" scheme. Some former Jeffersonian republics, such as Illinois, also followed that pattern after reorganization. Other reorganized states were captured by corporate interests and had to struggle against a fifth column of business officials within state government itself. California exemplified this "corporate captive" scenario. Finally, some Jeffersonian republics, such as Kansas, remained exactly that all the way through 1929.

In corporate liberal states, such as New York, business methods did not reduce spending; in fact, these methods often increased spending. Indeed, government research experts denied that the limitation of government had ever been their original intention at all. As one of the co-founders of the NYBMR put it, the government research movement was not "a penny-saving or penny-pinching proposition at all."[8] A 1916 publication of the NYBMR acknowledged that continuing expansion of government would be inevitable. "To attempt large reductions of taxes in this country is to attempt the impossible," it declared. "In almost every field of governmental activity, people are demanding more and better service . . . More and better service tends to increase the cost of government and that means more revenue must be paid into our public treasuries. Faced with a condition and not a theory, the bureau seeks to promote increased and improved government service."[9]

In corporate liberal states, the actual effects of business influence on government were less sinister than the phrase "corporate state" might imply. In most cases, state reorganization did not throw lunatics into the street or leave schoolchildren without desks. Draconian spending cuts were rare. For example, in a 1922 review of changes wrought by reorganization in the mental health care system of Illinois, welfare expert Henry C. Wright found little to complain about. Under the reorganized government, the department of welfare had no power to buy its own supplies or make improvements to its own buildings or facilities. Those powers resided in the office of the director of finance. Institution managers had to get the approval of that office before making any such purchases or improvements. The director of finance could reject or alter any such request. "In practice," however, noted Wright, "he seldom raises such questions." Wright also found "surprisingly few modifications" in the actual orders of the institutions. Indeed, "standards of food and care of patients were established not theretofore existing," including removal of bars from all windows.[10] In corporate liberal states such as Illinois, reorganization seemed to fulfill the promises of its prophets.

In other states, such as California, corporate influence seemed to have captured state government. In 1949, California journalist Franklin Hichborn recalled a particularly egregious example of corporation influence over the state legislature. In 1911, Hichborn mused, neither he nor any of his Progressive colleagues had really understood that the corporation tax would bring utility and financial companies "into State politics on an unheard of scale" and eventually create "a state machine in comparison with which the old Southern Pacific machine . . . was to become insignificant."[11] Hichborn sadly admitted that no one foresaw the "billion dollar lobby" of 1921 or the influence that corporate officials would attain in state agencies such as the board of equalization.

Yet even with its probusiness tax administration, the Golden State still managed to pass the tax increase of 1921, as well as the highway bond bill of 1919 and the teacher salary raise of 1920. Corporate resistance to tax increases did not stop California from continuing the trend toward higher spending for more public services.

Even in Kansas, the most die-hard Jeffersonian republic—which had never imposed a corporation tax or devoted a significant share of state revenue to education and underwent no reorganization movement before 1929—things changed between 1877 and 1929. Federal aid and gasoline taxation transformed its 1840s-vintage policy on internal improvements; by 1929, the Sunflower State was spending as much on highways per capita as New York and Pennsylvania.[12] As one farmer complained in 1928, state and local government in Kansas were riddled with "paternalistic and socialistic schemes" that included "municipal free concerts, free medical clinics, free city colleges, free dramatic entertainments, free golf courses, free tennis courts, free housekeeping advice, free cooking schools, free dressmaking assistance, free veterinary advice to farmers, free expert advice to various forms of industry, and above all free advice and service to agriculture by the carload." This farmer also complained about the "evil system of federal aid for local purposes," which had encouraged so much highway spending. "These schemes are agitated," he concluded, "not at farmers' meetings and conventions, but in business men's organizations," which were full of "semi-socialists and believers in paternalism . . . the most dangerous advocates of increased taxation." At least one Jeffersonian in Kansas was convinced that his state was well on the way toward corporate liberalism—or worse.[13]

The American debate over the role of government in Americans' lives would continue, but the rise of the corporate state had changed the terms of that debate forever. By the onset of the Great Depression, even many rural, agricultural states with small-government traditions—the Jeffersonian republics— were taking on characteristics of the corporate state. The rise of the corporate state between 1877 and 1929 established new levels of public services, new kinds of taxation, and new roles for business in government. New kinds of administrative machinery that incorporated business methods such as the executive budget and centralized purchasing and personnel standardized the business of government in most states. The business of government and the government of business had been transformed by the growth of public services, taxation, and the rise of the corporate state.

APPENDIX

FINANCIAL STATISTICS OF SELECTED STATES, 1877–1929

Data for New York, New Jersey, and Massachusetts, 1877 through 1929, are author's calculations based on reports of state treasurers and controllers. Data for Pennsylvania, 1877 through 1916, are author's calculations based on Richard E. Sylla, John B. Legler, and John Wallis, *Sources and Uses of Funds in State and Local Governments, 1790–1915* [machine-readable data set] (Ann Arbor, Mich.: Inter-University Consortium for Political and Social Research, 1995); hereafter cited as ICPSR data set 9728. Data for Pennsylvania, 1917 through 1929, are author's calculations based on U.S. Census, *Financial Statistics of States,* except where noted otherwise.

Data for Alabama and Tennessee, 1877 through 1914, and Mississippi, 1877 through 1915, are author's calculations based on ICPSR data set 9728. Data for Alabama and Tennessee, 1915 through 1929, and Mississippi, 1916 through 1929, are author's calculations based on US Census, *Financial Statistics of States,* except where noted otherwise. Tennessee data are annualized.

Data for Wisconsin, 1877 through 1914, are author's calculations based on reports of state treasurer. Data for Illinois, 1877 through 1914, and Michigan, 1877 through 1915, are author's calculations based on ICPSR data set 9728. Data for Illinois, 1915 through 1929, Michigan, 1916 through 1929, and Wisconsin, 1915 through 1929, are author's calculations based on U.S. Census, *Financial Statistics of States,* except where noted otherwise. Illinois data are annualized.

Data for North Dakota, 1877 through 1914, Kansas, 1877 through 1915, Nebraska, 1877 through 1916, and South Dakota, 1877 through 1917, are author's calculations based on ICPSR data set 9728. Data for North Dakota, 1915 through 1929, Kansas, 1916 through 1929, Nebraska, 1917 through 1929, and South Dakota, 1918 through 1929, are author's calculations based on U.S. Census, *Financial Statistics of States,* except where noted otherwise. Nebraska data are annualized.

Data for Oregon, Nevada, and California, 1877 through 1924, are author's calculations based on reports of state treasurers and controllers. Data for all three states, 1925 through 1929, were drawn from U.S. Census, *Financial Statistics of States.* Oregon data are annualized.

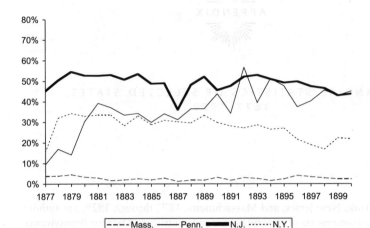

-- - -- Mass. ——— Penn. ━━━ N.J. ········ N.Y.

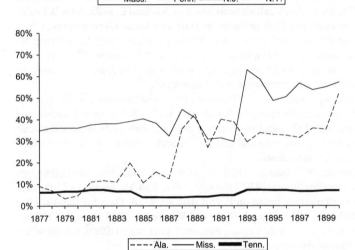

-- - -- Ala. ——— Miss. ━━━ Tenn.

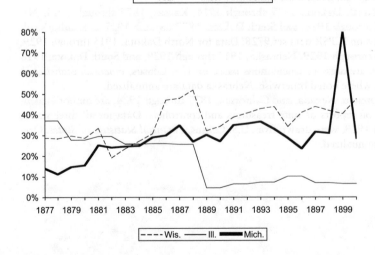

-- - -- Wis. ——— Ill. ━━━ Mich.

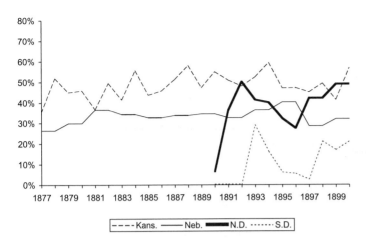

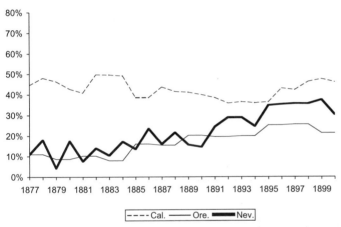

FIGURE 1. Education Spending as a Percentage of Total Annual Expenditures, 1877 to 1900

Notes: Mississippi data are interpolated for 1879, 1882, and 1883. Alabama data are interpolated for 1895. Tennessee data are interpolated for 1899–1900 biennium. Mississippi data from 1888 are based on report of state auditor. Illinois data are interpolated for 1885–86 biennium. North and South Dakota were admitted as states in 1889. South Dakota data are missing for 1890, 1891, and 1892.

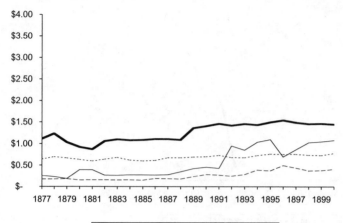

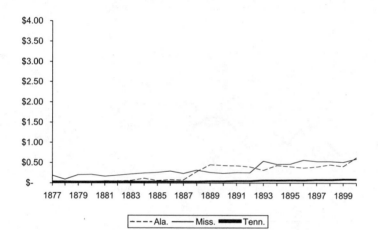

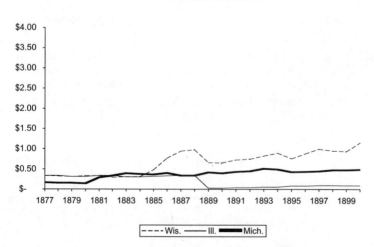

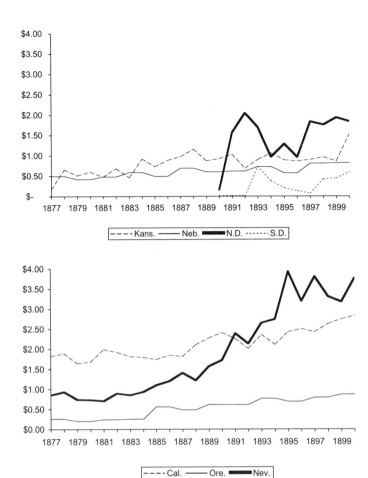

FIGURE 2. Annual Education Expenditures, 1877 to 1900 (in Real Dollars per Capita)

See notes to Figure 1.

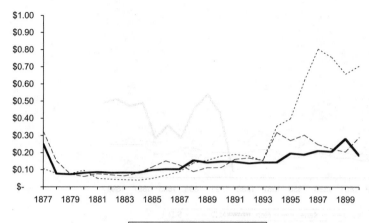

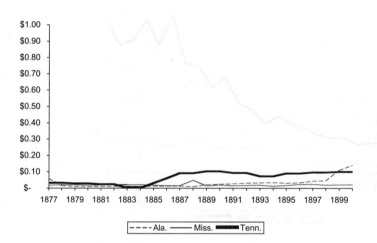

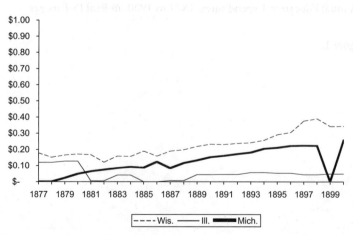

FIGURE 3. Annual Insane Asylum Expenditures, 1877 to 1900 (in Real Dollars per Capita)

Notes: See notes to Figure 1. Pennsylvania data are omitted because ICPSR data set 9728 shows no hospital expenditures, despite extensive secondary evidence to the contrary.

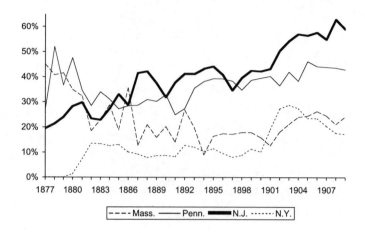

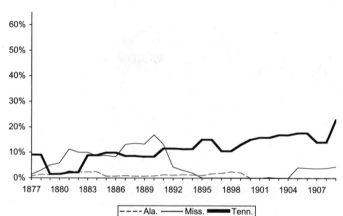

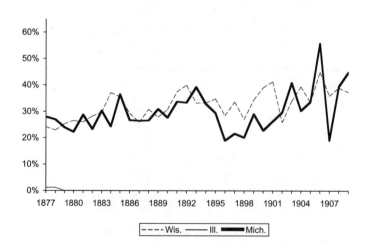

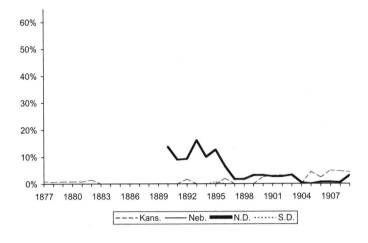

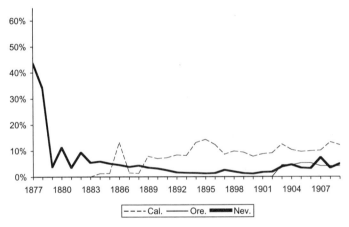

FIGURE 4. Corporation Tax Receipts as a Percentage of Total Annual Receipts, 1877 to 1909

See notes to Figure 1.

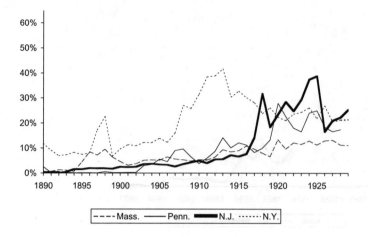

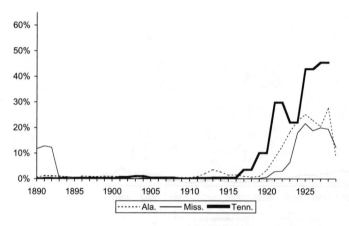

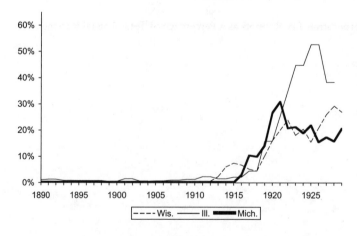

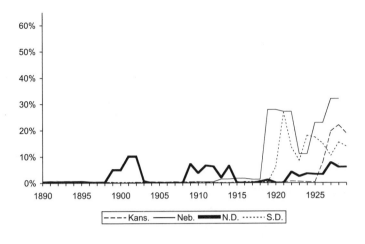

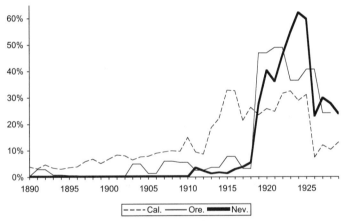

FIGURE 5. Transportation Spending as a Percentage of Total Annual Expenditures, 1890 to 1929

Notes: 1920 Pennsylvania data are based on report of state auditor. Alabama data for 1920 and 1921 are based on report of state auditor. Tennessee data for 1909, 1920, and 1921 are based on report of state comptroller. Mississippi data for 1920 and 1921 are based on report of state auditor. Wisconsin data are interpolated for 1920 and 1921; Illinois data are interpolated for the 1921–22 biennium. Michigan data for 1920 and 1921 are based on report of state auditor. Kansas data in 1920 and 1921 are based on report of state treasurer. Nebraska data for 1920 and 1921 are based on report of state auditor. South Dakota data for 1920 and 1921 are based on report of state treasurer. North Dakota data for 1904–8 and 1919–22 are based on report of state treasurer.

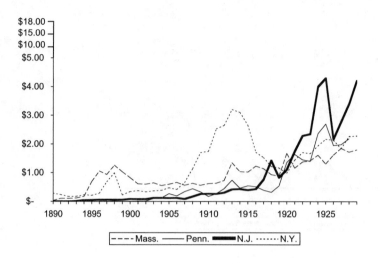

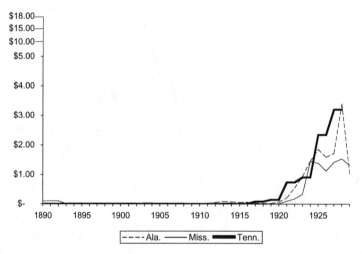

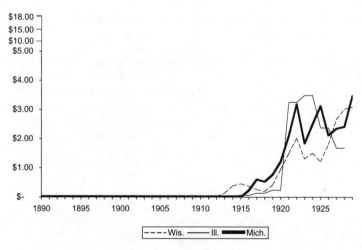

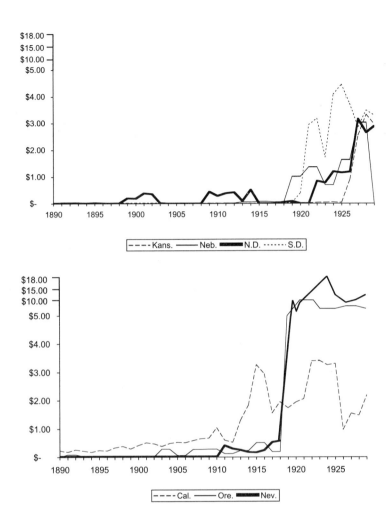

FIGURE 6. Annual Transportation Expenditures, 1890 to 1929 (in Real Dollars per Capita)

See notes to Figure 5.

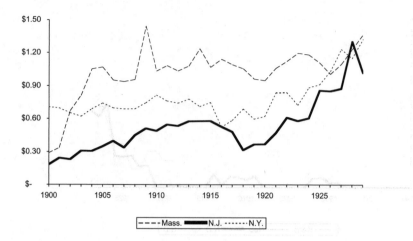

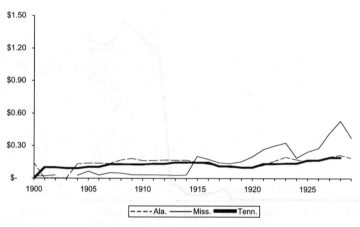

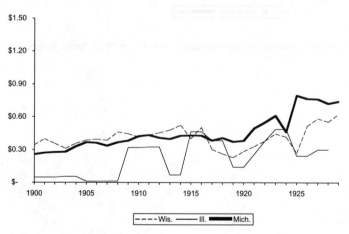

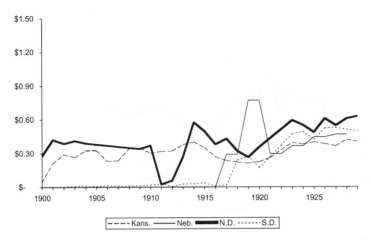

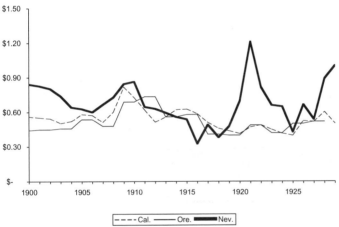

FIGURE 7. Annual Hospital Expenditures, 1900 to 1929 (in Real Dollars per Capita)

Notes: See notes to Figure 5. Pennsylvania data are omitted because ICPSR data set shows no hospital expenditures, despite extensive secondary evidence to the contrary.

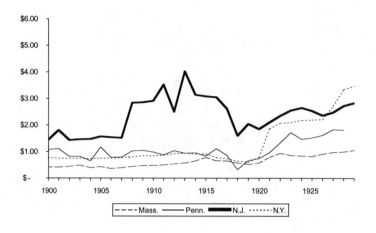

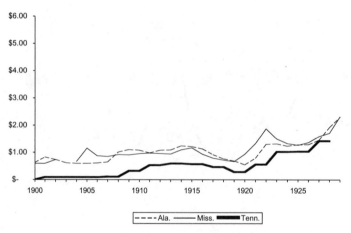

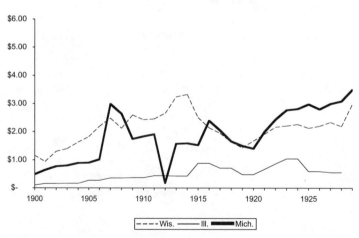

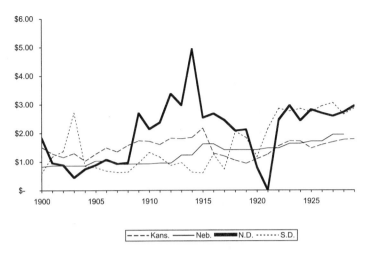

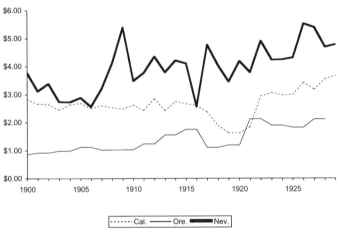

FIGURE 8. Annual Education Expenditures, 1900 to 1929 (in Real Dollars per Capita)

Notes: See notes to Figure 5.

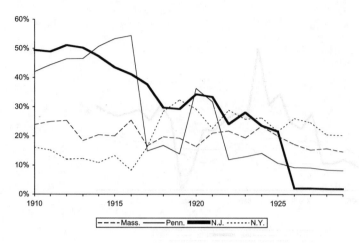

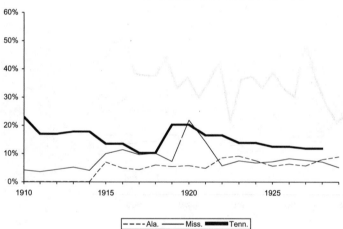

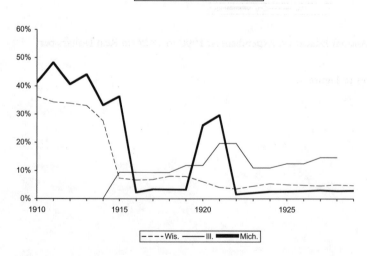

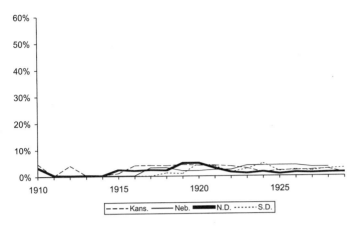

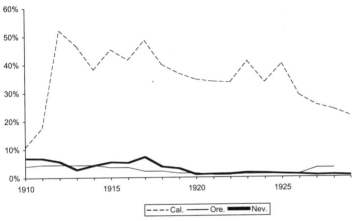

FIGURE 9. Corporation Tax Receipts as a Percentage of Total Annual Receipts, 1910 to 1929

See notes to Figure 5.

NOTES

INTRODUCTION

1. Alfred D. Chandler Jr., *The Visible Hand: The Managerial Revolution in American Business* (Cambridge, Mass.: Belknap Press, Harvard University Press, 1977).

2. Gabriel Kolko, *Railroads and Regulation, 1877–1916* (Westport, Conn.: Greenwood Press, 1965).

3. Naomi R. Lamoreaux, *The Great Merger Movement in American Business, 1895–1904* (New York: Cambridge University Press, 1985).

4. See, for example, James Weinstein, *The Corporate Ideal in the Liberal State: 1900–1918* (Boston: Beacon Press, 1968); Martin J. Sklar, *The Corporate Reconstruction of American Capitalism, 1890–1916* (New York: Cambridge University Press, 1988); Gerald Berk, "Corporate Liberalism Reconsidered: A Review Essay," *Journal of Policy History* 3, no. 1 (1991): 70–84.

5. Frederick W. Taylor, *The Principles of Scientific Management,* 1911 (New York: Norton, 1967).

6. Arthur Selwyn Miller, *The Modern Corporate State: Private Governments and the American Constitution,* Contributions in American Studies, no. 23 (Westport, Conn.: Greenwood Press, 1976), xiv, 28–29.

7. Robert H. Salisbury, "Why No Corporatism in America?" in *American Society and Politics,* ed. Theda Skocpol and J. C. Campbell (New York: McGraw Hill, 1995), 271–83; Colin Gordon, "Why No Corporatism in the United States? Business Disorganization and its Consequences," *Business and Economic History* 27, no. 1 (fall 1998): 29–46.

8. Ellis W. Hawley, "The Discovery and Study of a 'Corporate Liberalism,'" *Business History Review,* 52, no. 3 (autumn 1978): 309–20, repr. in Robert F. Himmelberg, *Business and Government in America Since 1870: A Twelve-Volume Anthology of Scholarly Articles,* vol. 5 (New York: Garland, 1994), 109–20.

9. James Bryce, *The American Commonwealth,* 3rd ed., vol. 1 (New York: Macmillan, 1906), 528.

10. R. Hal Williams, "The Politics of the Gilded Age," in *American Political History: Essays on the State of the Discipline,* ed. John F. Marszalek and Wilson D. Miscamble (Notre Dame, Ind.: University of Notre Dame Press, 1997), 117; Eric H. Monkkonen, *The Local State: Public Money and American Cities,* Stanford Studies in the New Political History (Stanford, Calif.: Stanford University Press, 1995), 10; Ballard Campbell, "Federalism, State Action, and 'Critical Episodes' in the Growth of

American Government," *Social Science History* 16, no. 4 (winter 1992): 561–77; idem, "Public Policy and State Government," in *The Gilded Age: Essays on the Origins of Modern America,* ed. Charles W. Calhoun (Wilmington, Del.: Scholarly Resources, 1996), 309–29; Morton Keller, *Affairs of State: Public Life in Late Nineteenth Century America* (Cambridge, Mass.: Belknap Press of Harvard University Press, 1977); William R. Brock, *Investigation and Responsibility: Public Responsibility in the United States, 1865–1900* (New York: Cambridge University Press, 1984).

11. "What—After All—Is 'Progressivism'?" *The Nation* 118:3058 (February 13, 1924): 160.

12. Eileen L. McDonagh, "Race, Class, and Gender in the Progressive Era: Restructuring State and Society," in *Progressivism and the New Democracy,* ed. Sidney M. Milkis and Jerome M. Mileur (Amherst: University of Massachusetts Press, 1999), 147.

13. Lynn Hudson Parsons, "The Hamiltonian Tradition in the United States, 1804–1912" (Ph.D. diss., Johns Hopkins University, 1967), 273, 279, 331.

14. Jane S. Dahlberg, *The New York Bureau of Municipal Research: Pioneer in Government Administration* (New York: New York University Press, 1966), vii.

15. Jeffrey Leigh Sedgwick, "Jeffersonianism in the Progressive Era," in Gary L. McDowell and Sharon L. Noble, *Reason and Republicanism: Thomas Jefferson's Legacy of Liberty* (Lanham, Md.: Rowman & Littlefield, 1997), 190.

16. Stephen Skowronek, *Building a New American State: The Expansion of National Administrative Capacities, 1877–1920* (Cambridge: Cambridge University Press, 1982); Theda Skocpol, *Protecting Soldiers and Mothers: The Political Origins of Social Policy in the United States* (Cambridge, Mass.: Belknap Press, Harvard University Press, 1992).

17. Elisabeth S. Clemens, *The People's Lobby: Organizational Innovation and the Rise of Interest Group Politics in the United States, 1890–1925* (Chicago: University of Chicago Press, 1997).

18. V. O. Key Jr. and Winston W. Crouch, *The Initiative and the Referendum in California,* Publications of the University of California at Los Angeles in Social Sciences (Berkeley: University of California Press, 1939).

19. Clemens in particular makes excellent tacit use of the notion of pluralism in her analysis, but Morton Keller's discussion is more explicit. Morton Keller, *Regulating a New Economy: Public Policy and Economic Change in America, 1900–1933* (Cambridge, Mass.: Harvard University Press, 1990), 3, 182.

20. U.S. Department of Commerce and Labor, Bureau of Corporations, *Taxation of Corporations Part I.—New England: Report on the System of Taxing Manufacturing, Mercantile, Transportation, and Transmission Corporations in the States of Maine, New Hampshire, Vermont, Massachusetts, Rhode Island, and Connecticut* (Washington, D.C.: Government Printing Office, 1909), 4.

21. Bryce, *American Commonwealth,* vol. 1, 512.

22. Ibid.

23. For the method of selecting states for inclusion in this study, see the Essay on Methods and Sources.

ONE: COMPROMISE, CORRUPTION, AND CONFRONTATION

1. Worth Robert Miller, "Farmers and Third-Party Politics," in *The Gilded Age: Essays on the Origins of Modern America,* ed. Charles W. Calhoun (Wilmington, Del.: Scholarly Resources, 1996): 235–60, 241–42.

2. Richard Hofstadter and Michael Wallace, eds., *American Violence: A Documentary History* (New York: Alfred A. Knopf, 1970), 133.

3. Mark Twain (Samuel L. Clemens) and Charles Dudley Warner, *The Gilded Age: A Tale of To-Day*, 1873 (Indianapolis: Bobbs-Merrill, 1972).

4. Because the election was finally decided by a special congressional commission in late January 1877 and approved by Congress after informal negotiations in February 1877, the deal was known as the Compromise of 1877, even though it settled the presidential election of 1876.

5. Edwin R. A. Seligman, "The General Property Tax," *Essays in Taxation*, 10th ed. (New York: Macmillan, 1928), 19–65; Clifton K. Yearley, *The Money Machines: The Breakdown and Reform of Governmental and Party Finance in the North, 1860–1920* (Albany: State University of New York Press, 1970); Morton Keller, *Affairs of State: Public Life in Late Nineteenth Century America* (Cambridge, Mass.: Belknap Press of Harvard University Press, 1977), 324; Glenn W. Fisher, *The Worst Tax? A History of the Property Tax in America*, Studies in Government and Public Policy (Lawrence: University Press of Kansas, 1996).

6. Edwin R. A. Seligman, "The Taxation of Corporations," in *Essays in Taxation*, 142–315, 152.

7. Louis Hartz, *Economic Policy and Democratic Thought: Pennsylvania, 1776–1860* (Cambridge, Mass.: Harvard University Press, 1948), 262–63.

8. Seligman, "Taxation of Corporations," 165, 195.

9. Ibid., 195; U.S. Department of Commerce and Labor, Bureau of Corporations, *Taxation of Corporations Part II—Middle Atlantic States: Report of the Commissioner of Corporations on the System of Taxing Manufacturing, Mercantile, Transportation, and Transmission Corporations in the States of New York, New Jersey, Pennsylvania, Delaware, and Maryland, and in the District of Columbia* (Washington, D.C.: Government Printing Office, 1910), 64. Hereafter cited as U.S. Bureau of Corporations, *Taxation of Corporations Part II.*

10. U.S. Bureau of Corporations, *Taxation of Corporations Part II*, 52.

11. The following summary of the Massachusetts corporation tax is based on Massachusetts Legislature, Commissioners Appointed to Inquire into the Expediency of Revising and Amending the Laws Relating to Taxation and Exemption Therefrom, *Report of the Commissioners . . . Relating to Taxation and Exemption Therefrom*, 1875, repr. as House Document no. 15, 1893 (Boston: Wright & Potter, 1893), 124–27 (hereafter cited as *Massachusetts 1875 Tax Report*), and U.S. Department of Commerce and Labor, Bureau of Corporations, *Taxation of Corporations Part I.—New England: Report on the System of Taxing Manufacturing, Mercantile, Transportation, and Transmission Corporations in the States of Maine, New Hampshire, Vermont, Massachusetts, Rhode Island, and Connecticut* (Washington, D.C.: Government Printing Office, 1909), 25, 85–90 (hereafter cited as U.S. Bureau of Corporations, *Taxation of Corporations Part I*).

12. Massachusetts Legislature, Commission Appointed to Inquire into the Expediency of Revising and Amending the Laws of the Commonwealth Relating to Taxation, *Report of the Commission* (Boston: Wright & Potter, 1897), 69.

13. Edwin R. A. Seligman, "American Reports on Taxation," in *Essays in Taxation*, 596–640, 598.

14. New York Legislature, *Report of the Commissioners Appointed by the Governor to Revise the Laws for the Assessment and Collection of Taxes*, Assembly Docu-

ments, 1871, vol. 3, no. 39 (Albany, N.Y.: Argus, 1871), 38. Hereafter cited as Wells Report.

15. Herbert Ronald Ferleger, *David A. Wells and the American Revenue System, 1865–1870* (Ann Arbor, Mich.: Edwards Brothers, 1942).

16. Wells Report, 17.

17. Ibid., 101.

18. Yearley, *Money Machines,* 172–73.

19. New York Legislature, *Report of the Commissioners to Revise the Statutes Relative to Taxation,* Senate Documents 1872, vol. 2, no. 26 (Albany, N.Y.: Argus, 1872), 13, 20.

20. Idem, *Report of the Joint Committee of the Senate and Assembly Relative to the Examination of the Subject of Taxation both for State and Local Purposes, Appointed in 1892, Pursuant to a Joint Resolution,* Assembly Documents 1893, vol. 13, no. 69 (Albany, N.Y.: James B. Lyon, 1893), 176 (hereafter cited as New York, Legislature, *1892 Tax Commission*); Massachusetts, Commission Appointed to Inquire into the Expediency of Revising and Amending the Laws of the Commonwealth Relating to Taxation, *Report of the Commission* (Boston: Wright & Potter, 1897), 68.

21. California, Controller, *Biennial Report of the Controller of the State of California, 23d and 24th Fiscal Years* (Sacramento: California State Printing Office, 1873), 15–16. Hereafter cited as California, *Controller's Report* (1873).

22. Michael R. Hyman, "Taxation, Public Policy, and Political Dissent: Yeoman Disaffection in the Post-Reconstruction Lower South," *Journal of Southern History* 55, no. 1 (February 1989): 49–76, 64.

23. "The Taxation of Personal Property," *The Nation,* February 10, 1881, 86–87.

24. New York State Assessors, *Report of the State Assessors for the Year 1873,* Senate Documents, 1874, vol. 2, no. 23 (Albany, N.Y.: Weed, Parsons, & Co., 1874), 8.

25. California, *Controller's Report* (1873), 19.

26. John W. Cadman Jr., *The Corporation in New Jersey: Business and Politics, 1791–1875* (Cambridge, Mass.: Harvard University Press, 1949), 55.

27. U.S. Department of Commerce and Labor, Bureau of Corporations, *Taxation of Corporations, Part III—Eastern Central States: Report of the Commissioner of Corporations on the System of Taxing Manufacturing, Mercantile, Transportation, and Transmission Corporations in the States of Ohio, Indiana, Illinois, Michigan, and Wisconsin* (Washington, D.C.: Government Printing Office, 1911), 79 (hereafter cited as U.S. Bureau of Corporations, *Taxation of Corporations Part III*).

28. Raymond V. Phelan, *The Financial History of Wisconsin* (Madison: University of Wisconsin, 1908), 33; W. Elliot Brownlee Jr., *Progressivism and Economic Growth: The Wisconsin Income Tax, 1911–1929* (Port Washington, N.Y.: Kennikat Press, 1974), 57.

29. Henry Adams, *The Education of Henry Adams: An Autobiography,* 1906 (Boston: Houghton Mifflin, 1927), 240.

30. For major accounts of the Granger movement to regulate railroads at the state level, see Solon J. Buck, *The Granger Movement: A Study of Agricultural Organization and its Political, Economic, and Social Manifestations, 1870–1880,* 1913 (Lincoln: University of Nebraska Press, 1963); Lee Benson, *Merchants, Farmers and Railroads: Railroad Regulation and New York Politics, 1850–1887* (Cambridge, Mass.: Harvard

University Press, 1955); George H. Miller, *Railroads and the Granger Laws* (Madison: University of Wisconsin Press, 1971); and Gabriel Kolko, *Railroads and Regulation: 1877 to 1916* (Westport, Conn.: Greenwood Press, 1965).

31. U.S. Bureau of Corporations, *Taxation of Corporations Part III,* 20, 57–61.

32. Ibid., 79.

33. James Ernest Boyle, "The Financial History of Kansas," *Bulletin of the University of Wisconsin Economics and Political Science Series* 5 (1908): 51; Hyman, "Taxation, Public Policy, and Political Dissent," 62–63.

34. Eric Foner, *Reconstruction: America's Unfinished Revolution, 1863–1877* (New York: Harper & Row, 1988), 379–92.

35. Hyman, "Taxation, Public Policy, and Political Dissent," 61–62.

36. 118 U.S. 394 (1886).

37. William C. Fankhauser, *A Financial History of California,* University of California Publications in Economics, ed. Adolph C. Miller, vol. 3, no. 2 (Berkeley: University of California Press, 1913): 101–408, 257–58; David Alan Johnson, *Founding the Far West: California, Oregon, and Nevada, 1840–1890* (Berkeley: University of California Press, 1992), 250–58; Bryce, vol. 2, 425–47.

38. Winfield J. Davis, *History of Political Conventions in California, 1849–1892,* Publications of the California State Library, 1 (Sacramento: California State Library, 1893), 366.

39. *New York Times,* April 16, 1880, 5.

40. Quoted in *New York Times,* May 24, 1879, 1.

41. Quoted in R. Hal Williams, *The Democratic Party and California Politics, 1880–1896* (Stanford, Calif.: Stanford University Press, 1973), 18.

42. Carl C. Plehn, "The General Property Tax in California," *Economic Studies* 2, no. 3 (June 1897): 119–95, 136, 178.

43. Ibid., 180; California Controller, *Biennial Report of the State Controller* (Sacramento: State Printing Office, 1882), 26.

44. California Controller, *Biennial Report of the State Controller* (1882), 24.

45. California State Board of Equalization, *Report of the State Board of Equalization* (Sacramento: State Printing Office, 1882), 11.

46. Ibid.

47. Ibid., 12.

48. Ibid., 14.

49. California Controller, *Biennial Report of the State Controller* (Sacramento: State Printing Office, 1884), 25.

50. Ibid.

51. Williams, 39.

52. California Board of Equalization, *Biennial Report* (1882), 13.

53. 116 U.S. 138 (1882).

54. Herbert Hovenkamp, *Enterprise and American Law, 1836–1937* (Cambridge, Mass.: Harvard University Press, 1991), 43–47; Morton J. Horwitz, "Santa Clara Revisited: The Development of Corporate Theory," *West Virginia Law Review* 88 (1985–86): 173–224.

55. Daniel W. Levy, "Classical Lawyers and the Southern Pacific Railroad," *Western Legal History* 9, no. 2 (summer/fall 1996): 177–226, 213–14.

56. Ibid., 216.

57. California Controller, *Biennial Report of the State Controller* (Sacramento: State Printing Office, 1888), 21.

58. California Controller, *Biennial Report of the State Controller* (Sacramento: State Printing Office, 1894), 25; Plehn, "General Property Tax," 180.

59. Plehn, "General Property Tax," 181.

TWO: PROGRESS, BIT BY BIT

1. California Controller, *Biennial Report of the State Controller* (1882), 24.

2. David Tyack and Thomas James, "State Government and American Public Education: Exploring the 'Primeval Forest,'" *History of Education Quarterly* 26, no. 1 (spring 1986): 39–69, 57–58.

3. Massachusetts Auditor, *Report of the Auditor of Accounts . . . for the Year Ending December 31, 1870* (Boston: Wright & Potter, 1871), footnote, 20.

4. New York Comptroller, *Special Report of the Comptroller upon the School Fund, and upon Taxation and Revenue,* Senate Documents 1885, vol. 5, no. 37 (Albany, N.Y.: Weed, Parsons & Co., 1885), 2.

5. Tyack and James, "State Government and American Public Education."

6. New York Comptroller, *Special Report* (1885), 3.

7. William C. Fankhauser, *A Financial History of California,* University of California Publications in Economics, ed. Adolph C. Miller, vol. 3, no. 2 (Berkeley: University of California Press, 1913): 101–408, 392.

8. Quoted in William Warren Ferrier, *Ninety Years of Education in California, 1846–1936: A Presentation of Educational Movements and their Outcome in Education Today* (Oakland, Calif.: West Coast Printing, 1937), 12.

9. New York Comptroller, *Special Report* (1885), 3.

10. James C. Mohr, "New York State's Free School Law of 1867: A Chapter in the Reconstruction of the North," *The New-York Historical Society Quarterly* 53, no. 3 (July 1969): 230–49.

11. Fankhauser, *Financial History of California,* 392.

12. Phelan, *Financial History of Wisconsin,* 186.

13. Quoted in Julian P. Boyd, ed., *Fundamental Laws and Constitutions of New Jersey, 1664–1964,* New Jersey Historical Series, vol. 17 (Princeton, N.J.: C. Van Nostrand, 1964), 175.

14. James P. Wickersham, "The Leading Characteristics of American Systems of Public Education," *The Addresses and Journal of Proceedings of the National Educational Association* (Salem, Ohio: Allan K. Tatem, 1881): 94–99, 96.

15. Carl F. Kaestle, *Pillars of the Republic: Common Schools and American Society, 1780–1860* (New York: Hill and Wang, 1983); Wiliam A. Link, *The Paradox of Southern Progressivism, 1880–1930,* Fred W. Morrison series in Southern Studies (Chapel Hill: University of North Carolina Press, 1992), 4.

16. Jacqueline Jones, *Soldiers of Light and Love: Northern Teachers and Georgia Blacks, 1865–1873* (Athens: University of Georgia Press, 1992).

17. Foner, *Reconstruction,* 366.

18. Hyman, "Taxation, Public Policy, and Political Dissent," 71.

19. U.S. Department of the Interior, *Report of the Commissioner of Education for the Year 1889–90,* vol. 1 (Washington, D.C.: Government Printing Office, 1893), 25.

20. See Appendix, Figure 1.

21. California Controller, *Biennial Report of the Controller of the State of California for the 27th and 28th Fiscal Years, Commencing July 1st, 1875, and Ending June 30th, 1877* (Sacramento: State Printing Office, 1877), 19.

22. Fankhauser, *Financial History of California*, 393.

23. See Appendix, Figure 2.

24. New York Legislature, *1892 Tax Commission*, 289.

25. The term *incrementalism* was invented by later political scientists to describe exactly this kind of spending growth, in which the previous year's expenditures determined the succeeding year's spending. Aaron Wildavsky, *The Politics of the Budgetary Process*, 3rd ed. (Boston: Little, Brown, and Co., 1979), 13.

26. Paul Starr, *The Social Transformation of American Medicine* (New York: Basic Books, 1982), 169; Gerald N. Grob, *Mental Illness and American Society, 1875–1940* (Princeton, N.J.: Princeton University Press, 1983), 82–92, 104–6; David J. Rothman, *Conscience and Convenience: The Asylum and its Alternatives in Progressive America* (Boston: Little, Brown and Co., 1980), 28. R. Rudy Higgens-Evenson, "The Political Asylum: State Making and the Medical Profession in Oregon, 1862–1900," *Pacific Northwest Quarterly* 89, no. 3 (summer 1998): 136–48; Russell Hollander, "Mental Health Policy in Washington Territory, 1853–1875," *Pacific Northwest Quarterly* 71, no. 4 (October 1980): 148–56.

27. David J. Rothman, *The Discovery of the Asylum: Social Order and Disorder in the New Republic* (Boston: Little, Brown and Co., 1971).

28. See Appendix, Figure 3.

29. Quoted in Edward J. Renehan Jr., *The Secret Six: The True Tale of the Men Who Conspired with John Brown* (New York: Crown Publishers, 1995), 109.

30. Edward Stanwood, "Memoir of Franklin Benjamin Sanborn," *Massachusetts Historical Society Proceedings* 51 (October 1917–June 1918): 307–11.

31. Thomas L. Haskell, *The Emergence of Professional Social Science: The American Social Science Association and the Nineteenth-Century Crisis of Authority* (Urbana: University of Illinois Press, 1977), 55, 99.

32. Renehan, *The Secret Six*, 263.

33. Haskell, *Emergence of Professional Social Science*, 135–38.

34. James C. Mohr, *Doctors and the Law: Medical Jurisprudence in Nineteenth-Century America* (Baltimore: Johns Hopkins University Press, 1996), 164–79.

35. Franklin B. Sanborn, *The Hospital Palace at Danvers: Argument of F. B. Sanborn before the Committee to Investigate the Cost of the Danvers Hospital, Friday, April 20, 1877* (n.p.: 1877), Massachusetts Historical Society, Boston, 1.

36. Boston *Globe* (morning), 4 February 1879, 2.

37. Ibid.

38. Boston *Daily Globe* (evening), 2 January 1879, 2.

39. Nathan Allen to John D. Long, November 28, 1879, Folder 5.17, Box 5, "General Correspondence, 1879," John D. Long Papers, Massachusetts Historical Society, Boston.

40. Frank B. Sanborn, *State Care versus State Custody*, repr. (Boston: George H. Ellis, 1900), 11.

41. Ibid., 12.

42. A. A. Chevaillier to John D. Long, November 1879, Folder 5.6, Box 5, "General Correspondence, 1879," John D. Long Papers, Massachusetts Historical Society, Boston, 2.

43. Sanborn, *Hospital Palace*, 5.

44. Charles Russell Codman, draft of letter to Fred'k A. Bradford, March 2, 1891, *Rough Drafts etc., Copies of Speeches & Letters by C. R. Codman (2nd of the name)*, manuscript volume in Charles Russell Codman Papers, Massachusetts Historical Society, Boston, 171.

45. New York Constitutional Convention Committee, *State and Local Government in New York*, Reports of Constitutional Convention Committee, vol. 4 (Albany, N.Y.: J. B. Lyon, 1938), 463.

46. New York Commission in Lunacy, *First Annual Report of the State Commission in Lunacy*, Assembly Documents 1890, vol. 8, no. 36 (Albany, N.Y.: James B. Lyon, 1890), 12, 32, 33.

47. Ibid., 34.

48. Ibid., 6.

49. *New York Times*, 16 April 1890, 4.

50. D. B. Eaton, "Notes and Recollections," *Proceedings of the Conference of Charities* (Detroit, May 1875), repr. in Sophonisba P. Breckinridge, *Public Welfare Administration in the United States: Select Documents*, University of Chicago Social Service Series (Chicago: University of Chicago, 1927), 355.

51. *New York Times*, April 16, 1890, 4.

52. Ibid.

53. New York Commission in Lunacy, *First Annual Report*, 69.

54. Ibid., 45, 54.

55. *New York Times*, 16 April 1890, 4.

56. Ibid.

57. New York Commission in Lunacy, *Second Annual Report*, Assembly Documents 1891, vol. 5, no. 24 (Albany, N.Y.: James B. Lyon, 1891), 41.

58. Quoted in ibid., 53.

59. Ibid., 54, 36.

60. Ibid., 59–60.

61. New York Comptroller, *Annual Report of the Comptroller*, Assembly Documents, vol. 1, no. 3 (Albany, N.Y.: James B. Lyon, 1894), xi.

62. Monroe County had already given up care of its insane in 1891. John Archibald Fairlie, *The Centralization of Administration in New York State*, Studies in History, Economics and Public Law, vol. 9, no. 3 (New York: Columbia University, 1898), 87. New York Governor, *Annual Message of the Governor*, Assembly Documents 1895 vol. 1, no. 2 (Albany, N.Y.: James B. Lyon, 1895), 8.

63. New York Comptroller, *Annual Report of the Comptroller*, Assembly Documents, vol. 1, no. 3 (Albany, N.Y.: Wynkoop Hallenbeck Crawford, 1896), v.

64. *New York Times*, 16 September 1895, 10.

THREE: FROM CHARTER-MONGERING TO CATCHING
CORPORATE FREELOADERS

1. See Elizabeth Sanders, *Roots of Reform: Farmers, Workers, and the American State 1877–1917* (Chicago: University of Chicago Press, 1999), 16–26; idem, "Industrial Concentration, Sectional Competition, and Antitrust Politics in America, 1880–1980," *Studies in American Political Development* 1 (1986): 142–214, 146–51;

Richard F. Bensel, *Sectionalism and American Political Development, 1880–1980* (Madison: University of Wisconsin Press, 1984), 37–57.

2. Kansas Governor, *Biennial Message of Jno. A. Martin, Governor, to the Legislature of Kansas, 1887* (Topeka: Kansas Publishing House, 1887), 13.

3. Boyle, "Financial History of Kansas," 66.

4. Seligman, "Taxation of Corporations," 176.

5. Ibid., 66.

6. New York Comptroller, *Annual Report of the Comptroller,* Assembly Documents, vol. 1, no. 3 (Albany, N.Y.: Weed, Parsons, and Co., 1881), 22.

7. New York State Assessors, *Report of the State Assessors,* Senate Documents 1881, vol. 1, no. 40 (Albany: Weed, Parsons, and Co., 1881), 12–13.

8. New York Comptroller, *Annual Report of the Comptroller* (1890), 14.

9. New York Comptroller, *Annual Report of the Comptroller,* Assembly Documents, vol. 1, no. 3 (Albany: Weed, Parsons, and Co., 1883), 28.

10. U.S. Bureau of Corporations, *Taxation of Corporations Part II,* 22; New York Governor, *Annual Message of the Governor,* Assembly Documents 1878, vol. 1, no. 2 (Albany, N.Y.: Jerome B. Parmenter, 1878), 5.

11. U.S. Bureau of Corporations, *Taxation of Corporations Part II,* 65.

12. For the fee, see Don C. Sowers, *The Financial History of New York State from 1789 to 1912,* Studies in History, Economics and Public Law, vol. 57, no. 2 (New York: Columbia University, 1914), 165.

13. Christopher Grandy, *New Jersey and the Fiscal Origins of Modern American Corporation Law* (New York: Garland, 1993).

14. U.S. Bureau of Corporations, *Taxation of Corporations Part II,* 36–50.

15. U.S. Bureau of Corporations, *Taxation of Corporations Part III,* 102.

16. David P. Thelen, *The New Citizenship: Origins of Progressivism in Wisconsin, 1885–1900* (Columbia: University of Missouri Press, 1972), 218–46.

17. Phelan, *Financial History of Wisconsin,* 205.

18. Ibid., 225–26.

19. Although the New Idea Republicans did not sponsor Wilson's initial run for governor in 1910, their support was crucial in his ultimate victory. See John Milton Cooper Jr., *The Warrior and the Priest: Woodrow Wilson and Theodore Roosevelt* (Cambridge, Mass.: Belknap Press of Harvard University Press, 1983), 168.

20. Ransom E. Noble Jr., *New Jersey Progressivism before Wilson,* Princeton Studies in History (Princeton, N.J.: Princeton University Press, 1946), 24–31; U.S. Bureau of Corporations, *Taxation of Corporations Part II,* 39.

21. Noble, *New Jersey Progressivism before Wilson,* 29.

22. "Summit Board of Trade Favors Repeal of Hillery Maximum Tax Rate Act," pamphlet, n.d., n.p., Gov. Edward C. Stokes Papers, Box 5, Folder 611c, New Jersey State Archives, Trenton.

23. U.S. Bureau of Corporations, *Taxation of Corporations Part II,* 46.

24. U.S. Bureau of Corporations, *Taxation of Corporations Part III,* 81, 21.

25. Robert Sherman La Forte, *Leaders of Reform: Progressive Republicans in Kansas, 1900–1916* (Lawrence: University Press of Kansas, 1974), 53.

26. Ibid., 85; Homer E. Socolofsky, *Kansas Governors* (Lawrence: University Press of Kansas, 1990), 137.

27. Kansas Tax Commission, *First Report of the Tax Commission* (Topeka: Kansas State Printing Office, 1908), 14.

28. Fisher, *The Worst Tax?* 132.

29. Kansas Tax Commission, *First Report,* 12.

30. Dewey W. Grantham, *Southern Progressivism: The Reconciliation of Progress and Tradition* (Knoxville: University of Tennessee Press, 1983), 143–54.

31. Frederic G. Young, "The Financial History of the State of Oregon," *Quarterly of the Oregon Historical Society* 10, no. 3 (September 1909): 263–95, 286.

32. California Controller, *Biennial Report of the State Controller* (Sacramento: State Printing Office, 1906), 30.

33. U.S. Bureau of Corporations, *Taxation of Corporations Part II,* 17; 12–13.

34. New York State Tax Commissioners, *Annual Report of the State Board of Tax Commissioners,* Senate Documents 1901, vol. 4, no. 22 (Albany, N.Y.: James B. Lyon, 1901), 7.

35. New York State Tax Commissioners, *Annual Report* (1901), 17.

36. Richard L. McCormick, *From Realignment to Reform: Political Change in New York State, 1893–1910* (Ithaca, N.Y.: Cornell University Press, 1981), 161–62.

37. Quoted in G. Wallace Chessman, *Governor Theodore Roosevelt: The Albany Apprenticeship, 1898–1900* (Cambridge, Mass.: Harvard University Press, 1965), 147.

38. New York Legislature, *Report of the Joint Committee on Taxation,* Senate Documents 1900, vol. 1, no. 7 (Albany, N.Y.: James B. Lyon, 1900), 13.

39. New York Comptroller, *Annual Report of the Comptroller,* Assembly Documents 1904, vol. 1, no. 4 (Albany, N.Y.: J. B. Lyon, 1904), xvi.

40. New York Legislature, *Report of the Joint Committee on Taxation* (1900), 13.

41. See Appendix, Figure 4.

42. Richard L. McCormick, "The Discovery that 'Business Corrupts Politics': A Reappraisal of the Origins of Progressivism," *American Historical Review* 86, no. 2 (April 1981): 247–74.

43. Albert Luther Ellis III, "The Regressive Era: Progressive Era Tax Reform and the National Tax Association—Roots of the Modern American Tax Structure" (Ph.D. diss., Rice University, 1991).

FOUR: THE SECOND ERA OF INTERNAL IMPROVEMENTS

1. John B. Rae, *The Road and the Car in American Life* (Cambridge, Mass.: MIT Press, 1971); Clay McShane, *Down the Asphalt Path: The Automobile and the American City* (New York: Columbia University Press, 1994); Sinclair Lewis, *Babbitt,* 1922 (New York: Signet, 1963), 19.

2. "An Outline of the History of Road Improvement in New Jersey," typescript, Gov. Franklin Murphy Correspondence, Box 2, File 25, New Jersey State Archives, Trenton. See also *New York Times,* 15 January 1892, 6.

3. M. O. Eldridge et al., "State Highway Management, Control, and Procedure (Continued)," *Public Roads* 1, no. 10 (February 1919): 30–102, 46.

4. Albert A. Pope to William E. Russell, Dec. 21, 1891, Folder 3.10, Box 3, "Correspondence, Sept.–Dec., 1891, " William E. Russell Papers, Massachusetts Historical Society, Boston.

5. Massachusetts Highway Commission, *Annual Report of the Massachusetts Highway Commission,* Public Document 54 (Boston: Wright & Potter, 1896), 6.

6. Massachusetts Auditor, *Report of the Auditor of Accounts . . . for the Year Ending December 31, 1895* (Boston: Wright & Potter, 1896), 563.

7. Massachusetts Auditor, *Report of the Auditor of Accounts . . . for the Year Ending December 31, 1894* (Boston: Wright & Potter, 1895), 535.

8. New York Governor, *Annual Message of the Governor,* Assembly Documents 1891 vol. 1, no. 2 (Albany, N.Y.: James B. Lyon, 1891), 17.

9. New York Governor, *Annual Message of the Governor,* Assembly Documents 1893 vol. 1, no. 2 (Albany, N.Y.: James B. Lyon, 1893), 41–42.

10. Paula Baker, *The Moral Frameworks of Public Life: Gender, Politics, and the State in Rural New York, 1870–1930* (New York: Oxford University Press, 1991), 104.

11. New York Governor, *Annual Message* (1893), 46.

12. *New York Times,* 22 April 1897, 4.

13. *New York Times,* 25 April 1897, 14.

14. Ballard Campbell, "The Good Roads Movement in Wisconsin, 1890–1911," *Wisconsin Magazine of History* 49 (summer 1966): 273–93.

15. *New York Times,* 17 March 1898, 3.

16. *New York Times,* 21 February 1898, 3.

17. Eldridge et al., "State Highway Management, Control, and Procedure," 51.

18. Baker, *Moral Frameworks of Public Life,* 105.

19. Charles L. Dearing and Adah H. Lee, "The Good Roads Movement," in Charles L. Dearing, *American Highway Policy* (Washington, D.C.: Brookings Institution, 1941), 219–65, 219.

20. Carter Goodrich, *Government Promotion of American Canals and Railroads, 1800–1890* (New York: Columbia University Press, 1960).

21. New York Constitutional Convention Committee, *Problems Relating to Taxation and Finance,* Reports of the Constitutional Convention Committee, vol. 10 (Albany, N.Y.: J. B. Lyon, 1938), 81.

22. Sowers, *Financial History of New York State,* 69.

23. James A. Roberts, *A Century in the Comptroller's Office* (Albany, N.Y.: James B. Lyon, 1897), 40; Noble E. Whitford, *History of the Canal System of the State of New York, Supplement to the Annual Report of the State Engineer and Surveyor . . . for the Fiscal Year Ending September 30, 1905,* 2 vols. (Albany, N.Y.: Brandow Printing Company, 1906), 169.

24. L. Ray Gunn, *The Decline of Authority: Public Economic Policy and Political Development in New York, 1800–1860* (Ithaca, N.Y.: Cornell University Press, 1988).

25. U.S. Bureau of Corporations, *Taxation of Corporations Part II,* 64.

26. Johnson, *Founding the Far West,* 102; Phelan, *Financial History of Wisconsin,* 11.

27. Whitford, *History of the Canal System of the State of New York,* 342.

28. Ibid.

29. Henry Wayland Hill, *Waterways and Canal Construction in New York State,* Buffalo Historical Society Publications, vol. 12, ed. Frank H. Severance (Buffalo: Buffalo Historical Society, 1908), 217.

30. Whitford, *History of the Canal System of the State of New York,* 344.

31. Hill, *Waterways and Canal Construction in New York State,* 228; Whitford, *History of the Canal System of the State of New York,* 350.

32. Whitford, *History of the Canal System of the State of New York,* 303.

33. New York Governor, *Message from the Governor Transmitting Report of the Canal Committee,* Assembly Documents 1900, vol. 19, no. 31 (Albany, N.Y.: James B. Lyon, 1900), iv.

34. New York Governor, *Annual Message* (1900), 6.

35. Michael J. McCarthy, "Governor Theodore Roosevelt's Canal Policies: Genesis of the New York State Barge Canal," paper presented at Theodore Roosevelt Conference, Sienna College, Londonville, New York, April 18, 1998, 22.

36. Whitford, *History of the Canal System of the State of New York,* 380.

37. Hill, *Waterways and Canal Construction in New York State,* 256.

38. Ibid., 318.

39. For details of the tax apportionment, see New York Legislature, *Report of the Committee on Canals,* 7, 32–33. For resistance of upstate counties, see Hill, *Waterways and Canal Construction in New York State,* 397.

40. Hill, *Waterways and Canal Construction in New York State,* 313.

41. Ibid., 268, 284.

42. McCormick, *From Realignment to Reform,* 150.

43. *New York Times,* Oct. 28, 1905, 8.

44. Eldridge et al., "State Highway Management, Control, and Procedure," 1918, 36; 1919, 68, 70, 97.

45. Benjamin U. Ratchford, *American State Debts,* 1941 (New York: Arno Press, 1966), 311.

46. San Francisco *Chronicle,* 28 January 1909, 3.

47. Commonwealth Club of California, "State Highway Act," *Transactions of the Commonwealth Club of California* 5, no. 7 (October 1910): 449–67, at 456.

48. San Francisco *Chronicle,* 6 January 1909, 3.

49. San Francisco *Chronicle,* 16 February 1909; 12 March 1909, 3.

50. San Francisco *Chronicle,* 2 November 1910.

51. San Francisco *Chronicle,* 2 February 1909, 3.

52. Commonwealth Club of California, "State Indebtedness," *Transactions of the Commonwealth Club of California* 3, no. 1 (January 1908): 1–25, 1–2.

53. Ben Blow, *California Highways: A Descriptive Record of Road Development by the State and by Such Counties as Have Paved Highways* (San Francisco: H. S. Crocker, 1920), 121–23; frontispiece.

54. Eldridge et al., "State Highway Management, Control, and Procedure," 1918, 50, 1919, 32, 42.

55. New York Governor, *Annual Message of the Governor,* Assembly Documents 1917, vol. 1, no. 2 (Albany, N.Y.: J. B. Lyon, 1917), 8.

56. Blow, *California Highways,* 7.

57. For example, in a 1919 cartoon titled "The Road to Riches," which was published in the San Francisco *Examiner* and the CSAA monthly *Motor Land,* a road in the shape of a dollar sign connects "California" (a redwood tree) with the rising sun of the "proposed state highways bond issue." See "Forty Million Dollar Highway Bond Issue," *Motor Land* 4, no. 4 (April 1919): 14–17, 17.

58. Austin B. Fletcher, "California's Road Program Financed," *Motor Land* 5, no. 2 (August 1919): 15–16.

59. Bruce E. Seely, *Building the American Highway System: Engineers as Policy Makers,* Technology and Urban Growth (Philadelphia: Temple University Press, 1987), 67.

60. Data for 1904 and 1914 are from *Public Roads* 3, no. 29 (September 1920): 12; data for 1926 and 1930 are from Dearing, *American Highway Policy,* 61.

61. New York Comptroller, *Annual Report of the Comptroller,* Assembly Documents, vol. 7, no. 10 (Albany, N.Y.: J. B. Lyon, 1918), xi.

62. Walter B. Brockway, "What Are the States Spending Money For?" *Proceedings of the Nineteenth Annual Conference on Taxation under the Auspices of the National Tax Association* (New York: National Tax Association, 1927): 252–65, 258.

63. State spending data in this paragraph are drawn from U.S. Department of Commerce, Bureau of the Census, *Historical Statistics on Governmental Finances and Employment* (Washington, D.C.: Government Printing Office, 1979), 51. State population data are drawn from idem, *Historical Statistics of the United States, Colonial Times to 1957* (Washington, D.C.: Government Printing Office, 1960), 8. Expenditures are expressed in 1902 dollars, deflated according to the Brady-David-Solar price index in John J. McCusker, "How Much Is That in Real Money? A Historical Price Index for Use as a Deflator of Money Values in the Economy of the United States," *Proceedings of the American Antiquarian Society* 101, no. 2 (1992): 297–373, 329–30.

64. See Appendix, Figure 5.

65. A. J. Brousseau, "A Billion for Highways! Who Pays the Bill?" *Nation's Business* 14, no. 1 (January 1926): 56–64, 60.

66. See Appendix, Figure 6.

67. Dearing, *American Highway Policy,* 266.

68. For a discussion of this general trend in American political history, see Mark L. Kornbluh, "From Participatory to Administrative Politics: A Social History of American Political Behavior, 1880–1918" (Ph.D. diss., Johns Hopkins University, 1987).

FIVE: CONSENT, CONTROL, AND CENTRALIZATION

1. Grob, *Mental Illness and American Society,* 69.

2. Fairlie, *Centralization of Administration in New York State,* 86.

3. Franklin B. Sanborn to Franklin Murphy, February 13, 1903, Gov. Franklin Murphy Correspondence, Box 9, File 233, New Jersey State Archives, Trenton, 2.

4. Breckinridge, *Public Welfare Administration in the United States,* 366–79.

5. Massachusetts Board of Lunacy and Charity, *Nineteenth Annual Report of the State Board of Lunacy and Charity,* Public Document 17 (Boston: Wright & Potter, 1898), 179.

6. Massachusetts State Board of Insanity, *First Annual Report of the State Board of Insanity,* Public Document 63 (Boston: Wright & Potter, 1900), 32.

7. Massachusetts Board of Insanity, *Second Annual Report of the State Board of Insanity,* Public Document 63 (Boston: Wright & Potter, 1901), 41.

8. Frank B. Sanborn, "State Care versus State Custody," *Report of the Proceedings of the 27th National Conference of Charities & Corrections,* repr. (Boston: George H. Ellis, 1900), 4.

9. Massachusetts Auditor, *Report of the Auditor of Accounts . . . for the Year Ending December 31, 1902* (Boston: Wright & Potter, 1903), 17–18.

10. Massachusetts, Auditor, "Statement IV.—Expenses of 1904 and 1905, etc.," *Report of the Auditor of Accounts . . . for the Year Ending December 31, 1905* (Boston: Wright & Potter, 1906), 141–56.

11. Boston *Globe* (evening), 8 January 1904, 8.

12. Republican Club of Massachusetts, *The New England Republican Primer, Or,*

A Safe and Sound Guide to the Art of Voting Right to which is added the Republican Catechism, Etc. (Boston: Republican Club of Massachusetts, 1905), 38–39.

13. Boston *Herald,* 5 January 1906, 1.

14. Massachusetts Auditor, *Report of the Auditor of Accounts . . . for the Year Ending November 30, 1909* (Boston: Wright & Potter, 1910), xix.

15. William Roscoe Thayer, "Memoir of Curtis Guild," Massachusetts Historical Society L (October 1916–June 1917), 308–12.

16. "Gov. Guild's Three Years," newspaper clipping, no title, scrapbook, Curtis Guild papers, Massachusetts Historical Society, Boston.

17. Massachusetts Treasurer, *Report of the Treasurer and Receiver-General for the Year Ending November 30, 1907* (Boston: Wright & Potter, 1908), 7.

18. Ellis, "The Regressive Era," 351–54.

19. Massachusetts Legislature, Joint Special Committee on Taxation Appointed to Consider the Expediency of Legislation in Amendment of or in Addition to the General Laws Relating to Taxation, *Report of the Joint Special Committee on Taxation,* House Document 1090 (Boston: Wright & Potter, 1907), 16–17.

20. California Governor, *First Biennial Message of Governor James H. Budd* (Sacramento: State Printing Office, 1897), 29.

21. California Commission in Lunacy, 3.

22. Ibid., 12.

23. California State Commission in Lunacy, *Seventh Biennial Report of the State Commission in Lunacy* (Sacramento: State Printing Office, 1910), 40.

24. Frances Cahn and Valeska Bary, *Welfare Activities of Federal, State, and Local governments in California, 1850–1934,* Publications of the Bureau of Public Administration (Berkeley: University of California Press, 1936), 193.

25. Massachusetts Commission on Mental Diseases, *Annual Report of the Massachusetts Commission on Mental Diseases,* Public Document 117 (Boston: Wright & Potter, 1919), 12.

26. New York Governor, *Annual Message of the Governor,* Legislative Documents 1919, vol. 1, no. 2 (Albany, N.Y.: J. B. Lyon, 1919), 14.

27. New York Legislature, *Report of the State Hospital Commission on the Needs for Additional Accommodations for the Insane,* Assembly Documents 1917 vol. 1, no. 6 (Albany, N.Y.: J. B. Lyon, 1917).

28. *New York Times,* 19 February 1923, 2.

29. Ibid.

30. *New York Times,* 14 March 1923, 3.

31. *New York Times,* 20 February 1923, 2, 16.

32. *New York Times,* 22 February 1923, 1.

33. *New York Times,* 31 October 1923, 28; 4 November 1923, 3.

34. *New York Times,* 30 October 1923, 21.

35. *New York Times,* 3 December 1923, 29.

36. New York Legislature, Special Joint Committee on Taxation and Retrenchment, *The Debt of the State of New York: Past, Present, and Future* (Albany, N.Y.: J. B. Lyon Company, Printers, 1926), 95.

37. See Appendix, Figure 7.

38. William A. Link, *The Paradox of Southern Progressivism, 1880–1930,* Fred W. Morrison series in Southern Studies (Chapel Hill: University of North Carolina Press, 1992), 142.

39. David Tyack, *The One Best System: A History of American Urban Education* (Cambridge, Mass.: Harvard University Press, 1974); Paul Theobald, *Call School: Rural Education in the Midwest to 1918* (Carbondale: Southern Illinois University Press, 1995).

40. Dewey W. Grantham, *Southern Progressivism: The Reconciliation of Progress and Tradition* (Knoxville: University of Tennessee Press, 1983), 252.

41. California Department of Education, *History of the California Textbook Plan* (Sacramento: State Printing Office, 1915), 6, 9.

42. California Controller, *Biennial Report of the State Controller* (Sacramento: State Printing Office, 1905), 23.

43. New York State Department of Education, "Elementary Education," *Annual Report*, vol. 2 (Albany: University of the State of New York, 1917), vii.

44. New York State Department of Education, *Annual Report* (Albany: University of the State of New York, 1926), 13.

45. New York Governor, *Annual Message of the Governor*, Legislative Documents 1919, vol. 1, no. 2 (Albany, N.Y.: J. B. Lyon, 1919), 5.

46. William G. Carr, *School Finance* (Palo Alto, Calif.: Stanford University Press, 1933), 17.

47. Massachusetts Department of Education, *Annual Report*, Public Document 2 (Boston: Wright & Potter, 1921), 21, 43, 45.

48. Portland *Oregonian*, 7 January 1920, 7.

49. V. O. Key Jr. and Winston W. Crouch, *The Initiative and the Referendum in California*, Publications of the University of California at Los Angeles in Social Sciences (Berkeley: University of California Press, 1939). 464.

50. New York State Department of Education, *Annual Report* (Albany: University of the State of New York, 1926), 15, 31.

51. See Appendix, Figure 8.

52. New York Legislature, Special Joint Committee on Taxation and Retrenchment, *Report of the Special Joint Committee on Taxation and Retrenchment Submitted February 15, 1925* (Albany, N.Y.: J. B. Lyon Company, Printers, 1925), 26–27.

SIX: GIANTS OF HISTORY

1. New York Legislature, *Report of the Special Tax Commission of the State of New York*, Senate Documents 1907, vol. 5, no. 11 (Albany, N.Y.: J. B. Lyon, 1907), 5.

2. California Controller *Biennial Report of the State Controller* (Sacramento: State Printing Office, 1905), 19.

3. Nicholas Murray Butler et al., *Edwin Robert Anderson Seligman, 1861–1939: Addresses Delivered at the Memorial Meeting Held on December the Thirteenth, 1939* (Stamford, Conn.: Overbrook Press, 1942).

4. Richard T. Ely, *Ground Under Our Feet: An Autobiography* (New York: Macmillan, 1938), 121.

5. Rodger Daniels, *Atlantic Crossings: Social Politics in a Progressive Age* (Cambridge, Mass.: Belknap Press of Harvard University Press, 1998), 103–5.

6. Edwin R. A. Seligman, *Essays in Taxation*, 10th ed. (New York: Macmillan, 1928), 57; Ellis, "The Regressive Era," 190.

7. Seligman, *Essays in Taxation*, 346–76.

8. Chessman, *Governor Theodore Roosevelt*, 141.

9. New York Legislature, *Report of the Joint Committee on Taxation,* Senate Documents 1900, vol. 1, no. 7 (Albany, N.Y.: James B. Lyon, 1900), 3.

10. New York Legislature, *Report of the Special Tax Commission,* 1907, 1, 8.

11. New York Legislature, *Report of the Joint Legislative Committee on Taxation,* Senate Documents, 1916, vol. 14, no. 26 (Albany, N.Y.: J. B. Lyon, 1916), 7.

12. Ellis, "The Regressive Era," 44.

13. Edwin R. A. Seligman, *The Income Tax: A Study of the History, Theory, and Practice of Income Taxation at Home and Abroad,* 2d ed., 1914, Reprints of Economic Classics (New York: Augustus M. Kelley, 1970), 416–17.

14. New York Legislature, *Report of the Joint Committee of the Senate and Assembly Relative to the Examination of the Subject of Taxation both for State and Local Purposes, Appointed in 1892, Pursuant to a Joint Resolution,* Assembly Documents 1893, vol. 13, no. 69 (Albany, N.Y.: James B. Lyon, 1893), 10.

15. W. Elliot Brownlee Jr., *Progressivism and Economic Growth: The Wisconsin Income Tax, 1911–1929* (Port Washington, N.Y.: Kennikat Press, 1974); John D. Buenker, *The Income Tax and the Progressive Era* (New York: Garland Publishing, 1985); Mansel G. Blackford, *The Politics of Business in California, 1890–1920* (Columbus: Ohio State University Press, 1977); Fisher, *The Worst Tax?* 160.

16. California Comptroller, *Biennial Report of the State Controller* (Sacramento: State Printing Office, 1908), 40.

17. California Comptroller, *Biennial Report of the State Controller* (Sacramento: State Printing Office, 1905), 19.

18. Carl C. Plehn, "The General Property Tax in California," *American Economic Association Economic Studies* 2, no. 3 (June 1897), 111–200.

19. Blackford, *Politics of Business in California,* 148–56.

20. Franklin Hichborn Papers, microfilm edition, *California Politics, 1891–1939* (Los Angeles: Haynes Foundation, 1949), 961.

21. California Commission on Revenue and Taxation, *Report,* 159.

22. Ibid., 12; emphasis in original.

23. Commonwealth Club of California, "The Proposed Taxation Amendments to the State Constitution," *Transactions of the Commonwealth Club of California* 3, no. 4 (May 1908): 93–192, 114, 131.

24. California Controller, *Biennial Report of the State Controller* (Sacramento: State Printing Office, 1912), 14.

25. Commonwealth Club of California, "Constitutional Amendments of 1910," *Transactions of the Commonwealth Club of California* 5, no. 6 (September 1910): 329–417, 348.

26. California State Board of Equalization, *Special Report of the California State Board of Equalization on the Relative Burden of State and Local Taxes in 1912* (Sacramento: State Printing Office, 1913), 5; Ray L. Riley, "The California Tax Problem," *Proceedings of the Twenty-First Annual Conference on Taxation Under the Auspices of the National Tax Association* (Columbia, S.C.: National Tax Association, 1929), 53–57, 54.

27. Edwin R. A. Seligman, "The Taxation of Corporations," *Essays in Taxation,* 9th ed. (New York: Macmillan, 1921), 142–315, 208.

28. Blackford, *Politics of Business in California,* 149.

29. Ellis, "The Regressive Era," 314.

30. See Appendix, Figures 7 and 8.

31. Ellis, "The Regressive Era," 350.

32. U.S. Department of Commerce, Bureau of Corporations, *Special Report on Taxation Supplementing Previous Reports on the Taxation of Corporations and Covering the Tax Movement Throughout the United States During 1912* (Washington, D.C.: Government Printing Office, 1914), 78.

33. Seligman, "Taxation of Corporations," 210.

34. Brownlee, *Progressivism and Economic Growth*, 40–59.

35. John H. Leenhouts, "Income Taxation and its Administrative Requirements," *Proceedings of the Twenty-First Annual Conference on Taxation Under the Auspices of the National Tax Association* (Columbia, S.C.: National Tax Association, 1929), 457–77, 460.

36. Seligman, "Taxation of Corporations," 210–11.

37. Edwin R. A. Seligman, "The Next Step in Tax Reform," in *Essays in Taxation,* 9th ed. (New York: Macmillan, 1921), 641–59, 643.

38. Sowers, *Financial History of New York State,* 147.

39. New York Governor, *Annual Message of the Governor,* Assembly Documents 1912, vol. 1, no. 2 (Albany, N.Y.: Argus, 1912), 6.

40. New York Comptroller, *Annual Report of the Comptroller,* Assembly Documents, vol. 2, no. 10 (Albany, N.Y.: J. B. Lyon, 1916), xi; *New York Times,* 21 February 1915, 1.

41. New York Legislature, *Report of the Joint Legislative Committee on Taxation,* Senate Documents, 1916, vol. 14, no. 26 (Albany, N.Y.: J. B. Lyon, 1916), 11.

42. Seligman, "Taxation of Corporations," 202.

43. New York Tax Department, *Seventh State Conference on Taxation, Rochester, New York, January 11 and 12, 1917, Addresses and Proceedings* (Albany, N.Y.: J. B. Lyon Company, Printers, 1917), 85.

44. La Forte, *Leaders of Reform,* 85.

45. Kansas Tax Commission, *Proceedings of the Fifth Biennial Conference Convention of the Tax Commission* (Topeka: Kansas State Printing Office, 1916), 9.

46. Kansas Tax Commission, *Eighth Biennial Report of the Tax Commission* (Topeka: Kansas State Printing Plant, 1922), 4.

47. Fisher, *The Worst Tax?* 152–53.

48. Kansas Tax Commission, *Proceedings of the Seventh Biennial Conference Convention* (Topeka: Kansas State Printing Plant, 1920), 69.

49. Ibid., 13.

50. Kansas Tax Commission, *Proceedings of the Tenth Biennial Conference Convention* (Topeka: Kansas State Printing Plant, 1926), 11.

51. Seligman, "Taxation of Corporations," 211, 214.

52. A. W. Kimball, "State Personal Income Taxes," *Proceedings of the Twenty-First Annual Conference on Taxation Under the Auspices of the National Tax Association* (Columbia, South Carolina: National Tax Association, 1929): 436–48, 437.

53. Brownlee, *Progressivism and Economic Growth,* 5.

54. See Appendix, Figure 9.

55. Because of apparent bookkeeping differences between state documents and U.S. Census reports, corporation tax receipts in Wisconsin, Michigan, and Pennsylvania are difficult to measure consistently over time.

56. John C. Burnham, "The Gasoline Tax and the Automobile Revolution," *Mississippi Valley Historical Review* 48, no. 3 (December 1961): 435–59.

57. Quoted in H. H. Ragle, "The Gasoline Tax and the Oil Industry," *Proceedings of the Twenty-Third Annual Conference on Taxation Under the Auspices of the National Tax Association* (Columbia, S.C.: National Tax Association, 1931), 167–73, 167.

58. Ibid., 168.

59. Burnham, "The Gasoline Tax and the Automobile Revolution," 449.

60. California State Board of Equalization, *Report of the State Board of Equalization for 1923 and 1924* (Sacramento: State Printing Office, 1924), 7.

SEVEN: THE TEST OF DEMOCRACY

1. Dahlberg, *New York Bureau of Municipal Research,* 4, 15; Jonathan Kahn, *Budgeting Democracy: State Building and Citizenship in America, 1890–1928* (Ithaca, N.Y.: Cornell University Press, 1997), 40, 45.

2. See, for example, New York State Tax Commissioners, *Annual Report of the State Board of Tax Commissioners,* Senate Documents 1916, vol. 3, no. 11 (Albany, N.Y.: J. B. Lyon, 1916), 12, 16, 17, 35.

3. New York Tax Department, *Third Conference of Local Assessors and Tenth State Conference on Taxation* (Albany, N.Y.: J. B. Lyon Company Printers, 1921), 160.

4. See, for example, California State Board of Equalization, *Report of the State Board of Equalization for 1907 and 1908* (Sacramento: State Printing Office, 1908), 17.

5. New York Tax Department, *First State Conference of Local Assessors and Sixth State Conference on Taxation* (Albany, N.Y.: J. B. Lyon Company, Printers, 1916), 31.

6. Kansas Tax Commission, *First Report of the Tax Commission* (Topeka: Kansas State Printing Office, 1908), 8.

7. California State Board of Equalization, *Report of the State Board of Equalization for 1909 and 1910* (Sacramento: State Printing Office, 1910), 101.

8. Quoted in Kansas Tax Commission, *Proceedings of the Tenth Biennial Conference Convention of Public Service Commission, Tax Department, and the County Assessors* (Topeka: Kansas State Printing Plant, 1926), 66.

9. Kansas Tax Commission, *Proceedings of the Eighth Biennial Conference Convention* (Topeka: Kansas State Printing Plant, 1922), 23.

10. Kansas Tax Commission, *Proceedings of the Third Biennial Conference Convention* (Topeka: Kansas State Printing Office, 1912), 103–6.

11. Kansas Tax Commission, *Proceedings of the Ninth Biennial Conference Convention* (Topeka: Kansas State Printing Plant, 1923), 33.

12. Ibid., 34.

13. Hichborn, *California Politics,* 971.

14. California State Board of Equalization, *Report of the State Board of Equalization for 1911 and 1912* (Sacramento: State Printing Office, 1912), 114.

15. California State Board of Equalization, *Report of the State Board of Equalization for 1919 and 1920* (Sacramento: State Printing Office, 1920), 70, 77.

16. California State Board of Equalization, *Report of the State Board of Equalization for 1913 and 1914* (Sacramento: State Printing Office, 1914), 28–29.

17. U.S. Department of Commerce and Labor, Bureau of Corporations, *Taxation of Corporations Part II,* 17.

18. New York Tax Department, *First State Conference of Local Assessors and Sixth State Conference on Taxation* (Albany, N.Y.: J. B. Lyon Company, Printers, 1916), 135–36.

19. Ibid., 141.

20. R. Hal Williams, *The Democratic Party and California Politics, 1880–1896* (Stanford, Calif.: Stanford University Press, 1973), 28.

21. McCormick, "The Discovery that 'Business Corrupts Politics.'"

22. Franklin Hichborn, *California Politics,* 1190.

23. California Controller, *Biennial Report of the State Controller* (1914), 11–13.

24. Hichborn, *California Politics,* 1433.

25. Hichborn, *California Politics,* 1790–94; California, Legislature, Tax Commission, *Final Report,* 141.

26. Hichborn, *California Politics,* 1825.

27. Ibid., 1835, fn. 5.

28. Ibid., 1854.

29. California State Board of Equalization, *Report of the State Board of Equalization for 1925 and 1926* (Sacramento: State Printing Office, 1926), 5.

30. New York Tax Department, *Third Conference of Local Assessors and Tenth State Conference on Taxation* (Albany, N.Y.: J. B. Lyon Company Printers, 1921), 160–61.

31. Dahlberg, *New York Bureau of Municipal Research,* vi.

32. Kahn, *Budgeting Democracy,* 46.

33. Norman N. Gill, *Municipal Research Bureaus: A Study of the Nation's Leading Citizen-Supported Agencies* (Washington, D.C.: American Council on Public Affairs, 1944), 24.

34. Harold A. Stone, "Governmental Research: An Explanation of the Research Department of California Taxpayers' Association," *Tax Digest* 8, no. 1 (January 1930): 24–27.

35. New York Tax Department, *Third Conference of Local Assessors and Tenth State Conference on Taxation,* 159, 160.

36. Thomas Schick, *The New York State Constitutional Convention of 1915 and the Modern State Governor* (Lebanon, Pa.: Sowers Printing, 1978), 23.

37. Frederick A. Cleveland and Arthur Eugene Buck, *The Budget and Responsible Government,* Introduction by William Howard Taft (New York: Macmillan, 1920), 93.

38. Dahlberg, *New York Bureau of Municipal Research,* 23, 101.

39. Schick, *New York State Constitutional Convention of 1915,* 38, 39, 53.

40. Dahlberg, *New York Bureau of Municipal Research,* 105–7.

41. Dahlberg, *New York Bureau of Municipal Research,* vii; Cleveland and Buck, xv.

42. Kahn, 60.

43. Cleveland and Buck, *The Budget and Responsible Government,* 152.

44. Breckinridge, *Public Welfare Administration in the United States,* ix.

45. A. E. Buck, *The Reorganization of State Governments in the United States* (New York: Columbia University Press for the National Municipal League, 1938), 152.

46. Ibid., 219–22.

47. Ibid., 204–8.

48. Morris Edwards, "Taxation and the Business Man: Work of National Chamber of Commerce for Economy in Public Expenditures Revealed," *Tax Digest* 7, no. 2 (February 1929): 52–54.

49. George Spalding, "Public Expenditures—Their Trend," *Proceedings of the Twenty-First Annual Conference on Taxation Under the Auspices of the National Tax Association* (Columbia, S.C.: National Tax Association, 1929), 76–95, 85.

50. Carl C. Plehn, "It's Spending Not Taxing That Counts," *Nation's Business* 12, no. 5 (May 1924): 13–15, 15.

51. Edward C. Delafield, "Facts of the Billion and a Half Dollar States Debt," *Annalist* 25 (June 22, 1925): 836.

52. National Industrial Conference Board, *State and Local Taxation of Business Corporations,* Studies in Taxation and Public Finance (New York: National Industrial Conference Board, 1931), 6.

53. "The Tax Burden on Corporations," *The Index* (June 1927): 6–7.

54. A. W. Shaw, "The Underlying Trend of Business," *System* 51, no. 4 (April 1927): 457–88, 488.

55. James Musatti, "Government with Relation to Business: Regulation and Taxation Affect Nation's Prosperity," *Tax Digest* 7, no. 4 (April 1929): 115–17.

56. Rolland A. Vandegrift, "How California Taxpayers' Association Uses Scientific Research in Budget Making," *Tax Digest* 7, no. 1 (January 1929): 7–27, 23.

57. Reinhold Hekeler, "Need of Uniformity in State Business Taxes," *Proceedings of the Eighteenth Annual Conference on Taxation Under the Auspices of the National Tax Association* (New York: National Tax Association, 1926), 188–211, 204.

58. Walter B. Brockway, "What Are the States Spending Money For?" *Proceedings of the Nineteenth Annual Conference on Taxation Under the Auspices of the National Tax Association* (New York: National Tax Association, 1927), 252–79, 271, 272.

CONCLUSION

1. New York Tax Department, *Seventh Conference of Local Assessors and Fourteenth State Conference on Taxation* (Albany, N.Y.: J. B. Lyon Co., 1930), 70.

2. Philip J. Ethington, "The Metropolis and Multicultural Ethics: Direct Democracy versus Deliberative Democracy in the Progressive Era," in *Progressivism and the New Democracy,* ed. Sidney M. Milkis and Jerome M. Mileur (Amherst: University of Massachusetts Press, 1999), 192–225.

3. Hill, *Waterways and Canal Construction in New York State,* 389–90.

4. Elisabeth S. Clemens, *The People's Lobby.*

5. Key and Crouch, *The Initiative and the Referendum in California,* 572.

6. Ibid., 573.

7. New York Legislature, Special Joint Committee on Taxation and Retrenchment, *State Expenditures, Tax Burden, and Wealth: A Study of the Growth of the Functions and Expenditures of the State Government and the Relation of Total Tax Burden to the Income of the People of the State* (Albany, N.Y.: J. B. Lyon Co., 1926), 51.

8. Dahlberg, *New York Bureau of Municipal Research,* 32.

9. Quoted in Gill, *Municipal Research Bureaus,* 35.

10. Henry C. Wright, *A Valuation of a System for the Administration of the State Institutions as Operated in Illinois, Made for the New York State Charities Aid Association* (1922), repr. in Sophonisba P. Breckinridge, *Public Welfare Administration in the United States: Select Documents,* 2d ed. (Chicago: University of Chicago Press, 1938), 573–77.

11. Hichborn, *California Politics,* 1070.

12. See Appendix, Figures 5 and 6.

13. Rodney A. Elward, "You Business Men Are Making Taxes High!" *Nation's Business* 16, no. 8 (July 1928): 15–16, 94–96.

In this exploration of state fiscal history, I have relied on quantitative and qualitative evidence. The best sources of quantitative data on state spending are annual or biennial reports of state financial officers. There typically are two such officials: the treasurer and the auditor (also known as the controller or comptroller). The reports of the latter official usually are more useful because the numbers have been organized. Treasurers' reports tend merely to list expenditures and receipts in no particular order. In the worst cases, they read like checkbook registers, simply listing every warrant for payment written on a state account during the previous fiscal year. Auditors' reports, on the other hand, were supposed to be used by the legislature in making appropriations for the upcoming year, so they usually categorized the previous year's receipts and expenditures in a more useful way.

Because every state categorized receipts and expenditures differently, those documents are extremely difficult to compare across states. To overcome this problem, I chose the most concise tabulation in each report, photocopied it, and transcribed it onto a spreadsheet. I then reclassified each spreadsheet according to the categories in U.S. Department of Commerce, Bureau of the Census, *Wealth, Debt, and Taxation,* vol. 2 (Washington, D.C.: Government Printing Office, 1915), 21–25. Those categories are the same as those used in U.S. Department of Commerce, Bureau of the Census, *Financial Statistics of States* (Washington, D.C.: Government Printing Office, 1915 through 1929, except 1920 and 1921)—the standard twentieth-century source for state financial statistics. Because the reclassification of expenditures and receipts was so time-consuming and labor-intensive, I only used this method with seven states: New York, New Jersey, Massachusetts, California, Nevada, Oregon, and Wisconsin.

Only two other sources of state fiscal data exist, aside from published reports of state officials before 1915 and the U.S. Census *Financial Statistics of*

States series for 1915 and later years. The first—Charles Frank Holt, *The Role of State Government in the Nineteenth Century American Economy, 1820–1902: A Quantitative Study* (New York: Arno Press, 1977)—includes an appendix enumerating state revenues and expenditures. Because Holt estimated a significant proportion of his figures, however, they contain too many flaws to be used as the basis for serious research. The other compilation of state fiscal data, which is more accurate and more easily manipulated by computer, is Richard E. Sylla, John B. Legler, and John Wallis, *Sources and Uses of Funds in State and Local Governments, 1790–1915* [computer file] (New York: Richard E. Sylla, New York University; Athens, Ga.: John B. Legler, University of Georgia; College Park, Md.: John Wallis, University of Maryland [producers], 1994; Ann Arbor, Mich.: Inter-university Consortium for Political and Social Research (ICPSR) [distributor], 1995). ICPSR data set 9728, however, still contains several serious lacunae, and its classification scheme sometimes is inconsistent.

I selected a nationwide sample of states on the basis of three criteria: fiscal policy innovations, geographic and economic diversity, and quality of available data. The first criterion dictated the selection of New York, Massachusetts, Wisconsin, Pennsylvania, and California. The second criterion suggested including immediate neighbors of those states, such as New Jersey, Oregon, and Nevada. In addition, I wanted some "control" states that had no notable policy innovations, as well as states from every geographical region. I selected the following states on the basis of the quality of the data available in ICPSR data set 9728: Mississippi, Alabama, Tennessee, Michigan, Illinois, North Dakota, South Dakota, Kansas, and Nebraska. In several cases—notably Mississippi and North Dakota—the ICPSR data set had numerous holes. I filled these in as well as I could by using published reports of state officials whenever available, but some data remain missing.

For the seven states on which I collected data from the reports of state officials, I transcribed data from 1877 through 1929. (Wisconsin was an exception: I used U.S. Bureau of the Census, *Financial Statistics of States,* for Wisconsin from 1915 onward.) For the ICPSR data set states, I used *Financial Statistics of States* for the years from 1915 onward. For the years 1920 and 1921, the Census Bureau did not publish *Financial Statistics of States,* so I filled in where I could from the reports of state officials. Some data remain lacking.

The combination of data from three different sources—ICPSR data set 9728, *Financial Statistics of States,* and reports of state officials—shows some differences among the three methods of bookkeeping. The data for Pennsylvania in particular suffer from inconsistencies that appear to be artifacts of bookkeeping discrepancies among the three sources. Although the ideal solution would be to generate a new data set with a consistent scheme of reclassification, such a project would be prohibitively costly. The data on which this study stand are imperfect, but a cross-check between my results for the seven states I transcribed and ICPSR data set 9728 suggests that the data are reliable, for the most part, until the 1915 transition to the Census Bureau data. Data for New York, New Jersey, Massachusetts, Nevada, Oregon, and California are reliable for the entire period because they were all drawn from reports of state officials.

Because this study is exploratory rather than hypothesis-testing, I have used only the simplest descriptive statistics. Future studies might use inferential techniques to test the relationship between various kinds of expenditures and receipts, but the weakness of contemporaneous data on other independent variables such as state wealth will make such projects difficult. To convert current dollar values to real dollars, I used the Brady-David-Solar (BDS) price index from John J. McCusker, "How Much is that in Real Money? A Historical Price Index for Use as a Deflator of Money Values in the Economy of the United States," *Proceedings of the American Antiquarian Society* 101, no. 2 (1992): 297–373, 328–330. I used 1900 as the index year, partly because it falls in the center of my period of study and partly because the price index reached unity then. I calculated per capita figures by using annual state populations interpolated from commonly available decennial census numbers.

After reviewing the data, I chose the three largest areas of spending policy and the three largest sources of receipts for further analysis. States far and away spent the most on education. Highways came in a close second, especially in the late 1920s, and hospitals were a distant third. Other areas of state policy—such as corrections and law enforcement, parks and recreation, and natural resources—accounted for much smaller shares of public resources. For most states, property taxes were the largest source of receipts, followed by the corporation tax and bond sales. By the 1920s, the latter source had become predominant.

In analyzing the quantitative data for this study, I read extensively in primary qualitative sources for three major states—New York, Massachusetts, and California—visiting archival collections in each one. For the remainder of the states, I relied mainly on secondary sources.

Among primary sources, I turned first to text reports that accompanied tabulated numbers in annual reports of state auditors and controllers. Those officials, who oversaw daily deposits and withdrawals from the state's funds, advised legislators and administrators, and always kept one eye on the political horizon, were at the center of state fiscal policy. Their reports were the single most valuable primary source for this study.

The next most valuable state documents were annual messages of the governor. Gubernatorial speeches usually touched on the most important political issues of the day and often provided valuable perspective on events described but not fully explained by the controller.

The third type of public document I found most useful consisted of annual reports of state tax commissions, boards of equalization, or assessors. These agencies were responsible for day-to-day administration of state tax laws. They considered possible revisions, held hearings, calculated an equalized tax rate for the entire state, and assessed property. Their value as a primary source is very uneven. Some agencies provided detailed commentary on the year's activities; others merely dashed off a summary paragraph before proceeding to tabulated data. New York Legislature, *Report of the Joint Committee of the Senate and Assembly Relative to the Examination of the Subject of Taxation both for State and Local Purposes, Appointed in 1892, Pursuant to a Joint Resolution,* Assembly Documents 1893, vol. 13, no. 69 (Albany: James B. Lyon, 1893) is a particularly outstanding example of this type of source, weighing in with almost 600 pages of testimony from New York businessmen about the impact of state corporation taxes.

I turned to newspapers only after learning the dates of significant fiscal events from published reports of state officials. Newspaper accounts were most useful in providing political background behind particular laws or movements.

State archives and personal papers were surprisingly unhelpful. State officials tended to put the most important information in their published reports. In most cases, the working papers of nineteenth-century state officials do not survive, having been removed from the office by outgoing officials or destroyed in fires such as the one that burned most of the nineteenth-century records in the New York State Archives in 1911. The most valuable archival documents for this project were in an unlabeled newspaper scrapbook in the Curtis Guild papers, Massachusetts Historical Society, Boston, and in the Governor Edward C. Stokes Papers, New Jersey State Archives, Trenton.

U.S. Department of Commerce and Labor, Bureau of Corporations, *Taxation of Corporations Part I.—New England: Report on the System of Taxing Manufacturing, Mercantile, Transportation, and Transmission Corporations in the States of Maine, New Hampshire, Vermont, Massachusetts, Rhode Is-*

land, and Connecticut (Washington, D.C.: Government Printing Office, 1909), and its two sequels, published in 1910 and 1911 and dealing with the middle Atlantic and midwestern states, respectively, provide the single most useful source on state corporation taxes as they existed on the eve of the income tax revolution. Written for a lay audience, those reports not only provide clear, concise, and readable summaries of corporation tax laws state by state; they also often give a historical précis of the development of the corporation tax in each state. Their historical summaries make these reports more useful than National Industrial Conference Board, *State and Local Taxation of Business Corporations,* Studies in Taxation and Public Finance (New York: National Industrial Conference Board, 1931).

For insights into the corporate response to taxation, I turned to three major sources. For the years from 1907 to 1929, the annual *Proceedings* of the National Tax Association provide an excellent glimpse into the heads of businessmen and state tax officials as they grappled with the everyday problems of paying the price of progress. Likewise, the publications of individual state taxpayers' associations, such as *The Tax Digest* (California), provide monthly reviews of state tax policy from a business perspective. For the years from 1914 to 1929, *The Industrial Arts Index* (New York: H. W. Wilson) provides an invaluable annual guide, organized by topic, to articles in business periodicals. In addition to those sources, the National Industrial Conference Board's series, *Cost of Government in the United States* (New York: National Industrial Conference Board), for the years from 1926 to 1929, provides a useful tabulation of state finances but is largely based on *Financial Statistics of States.*

For historical overviews of state financial policy, state fiscal histories published in the 1910s are unbeatable. Particularly useful are James Ernest Boyle, "The Financial History of Kansas," *Bulletin of the University of Wisconsin Economics and Political Science Series 5* (1908): 1–179; Raymond V. Phelan, *The Financial History of Wisconsin* (Madison: University of Wisconsin, 1908), repr. *Bulletin of the University of Wisconsin Economics and Political Science Series,* vol. 2, pp. 183–475; William C. Fankhauser, *A Financial History of California,* University of California Publications in Economics, ed. Adolph C. Miller, vol. 3, no. 2 (Berkeley: University of California Press, 1913), 101–408; and Don C. Sowers, *The Financial History of New York State from 1789 to 1912,* Studies in History, Economics and Public Law, vol. 57, no. 2 (New York: Columbia University, 1914).

In researching specific policy areas, I turned first to relevant reports of the state agencies in charge. Annual reports of the state superintendent of instruction detailed the year's most important events in education policy. For nation-wide statistics on state school systems, especially data on local and state spending, annual reports of the U.S. Commissioner of Education (Department of the Interior) were extremely useful. Annual reports of managers of various institutions also were helpful, although more cumbersome and less valuable than summaries in annual reports of state boards of charities and corrections, most of which were reorganized as departments of institutions after 1917. Annual reports of state highway departments outlined developments in that area, although I found secondary sources on highway development that were more useful. These secondary sources included Charles L. Dearing, *American Highway Policy* (Washington, D.C.: Brookings Institution, 1941), and the U.S. Department of Agriculture Bureau of Public Roads magazine, *Public Roads,* 1918 and 1919 series on state highway policy, which included a historical synopsis for each state.

The most useful later secondary sources include Edwin R. A. Seligman's classic *Essays in Taxation,* 10th ed. (New York: Macmillan, 1928), which provides state-by-state summaries that are almost as good as the 1909–1911 Bureau of Corporations reports. Clifton K. Yearley's account, *The Money Machines: The Breakdown and Reform of Governmental and Party Finance in the North, 1860–1920* (Albany: State University of New York Press, 1970), remains the standard on the subject, although Yearley lacks sufficient evidence to sustain his argument that an unofficial machinery of partisan graft contributed to the "collapse" of fiscal machinery in the Northeast. More sharply focused state-level studies of the relationship between taxation and big business, generally written from a Gabriel Kolko-style revisionist perspective that assumes that big business sought taxation for its own purposes, have become minor classics in their own right: David P. Thelen, *The New Citizenship: Origins of Progressivism in Wisconsin, 1885–1900* (Columbia: University of Missouri Press, 1972); W. Elliot Brownlee, Jr. *Progressivism and Economic Growth: The Wisconsin Income Tax, 1911–1929* (Port Washington, N.Y.: Kennikat Press, 1974); Mansel G. Blackford, *The Politics of Business in California, 1890–1920* (Columbus: Ohio State University Press, 1977).

Christopher Grandy, *New Jersey and the Fiscal Origins of Modern American Corporation Law* (New York: Garland, 1993), serves as a bridge between the older revisionist studies and the state-centered institutional approach apparent in urban histories such as Terrence J. McDonald, *The Parameters of Urban Fiscal Policy: Socioeconomic Change and Political Culture in San Francisco, 1860–1906* (Berkeley: University of California Press, 1986); Jon C.

Teaford, *The Unheralded Triumph: City Government in America, 1870–1900* (Baltimore: Johns Hopkins University Press, 1984); and Eric H. Monkkonen, *The Local State: Public Money and American Cities,* Stanford Studies in the New Political History (Stanford, Calif.: Stanford University Press, 1995). These studies emphasize the demands of government administration itself as a causal factor in political history—a theoretical approach I have found particularly useful.

Although they contain useful empirical material, Glenn W. Fisher, *The Worst Tax? A History of the Property Tax in America,* Studies in Government and Public Policy (Lawrence: University Press of Kansas, 1996), and Albert Luther Ellis III, "The Regressive Era: Progressive Era Tax Reform and the National Tax Association—Roots of the Modern American Tax Structure" (Ph.D. diss., Rice University, 1991), seem to have wandered down the path of trying to justify a universal return to the property tax.

For background on federal income and corporation tax, I turned to John D. Buenker, *The Income Tax and the Progressive Era* (New York: Garland Publishing, 1985), and W. Elliot Brownlee's intriguing *Federal Taxation in America: A Short History* (Cambridge, England: Cambridge University Press, 1996).

For background on highway policy, I relied on John C. Burnham, "The Gasoline Tax and the Automobile Revolution," *Mississippi Valley Historical Review* 48, no. 3 (December 1961): 435–459; John B. Rae, *The Road and the Car in American Life* (Cambridge, Mass.: MIT Press, 1971); Clay McShane, *Down the Asphalt Path: The Automobile and the American City* (New York: Columbia University Press, 1994); and Bruce E. Seely, *Building the American Highway System: Engineers as Policy Makers,* Technology and Urban Growth (Philadelphia: Temple University Press, 1987).

On education policy, David Tyack and Thomas James, "State Government and American Public Education: Exploring the 'Primeval Forest,'" *History of Education Quarterly* 26, no. 1 (spring 1986): 39–69, provides a good starting point for research on the role of state government in particular. For background on educational development in general during this period, see David Tyack, *The One Best System: A History of American Urban Education* (Cambridge, Mass.: Harvard University Press, 1974), and Paul Theobald, *Call School: Rural Education in the Midwest to 1918* (Carbondale: Southern Illinois University Press, 1995).

For the role of states in developing mental health care policy, I turned for background to James C. Mohr, *Doctors and the Law: Medical Jurisprudence in Nineteenth-Century America* (Baltimore: The Johns Hopkins University Press, 1996); Gerald N. Grob, *Mental Illness and American Society, 1875–1940* (Princeton, N.J.: Princeton University Press, 1983); and David J. Rothman, *Conscience and Convenience: The Asylum and its Alternatives in Progressive America* (Boston: Little, Brown and Co., 1980).

In conceptualizing the relationship between state and society, especially state and business, between 1877 and 1929, I generally subscribe to the "organizational synthesis" school begun by Robert Wiebe, *The Search for Order, 1877–1920* (New York: Hill and Wang, 1967), and continued in Louis Galambos, "The Emerging Organizational Synthesis in Modern American History," *Business History Review* 44, no. 3 (autumn 1970): 279–90; idem, "Technology, Political Economy, and Professionalization: Central Themes of the Organizational Synthesis," *Business History Review* 57, no. 4 (winter 1983): 471–93; Ellis Hawley, The Great War and the Search for a Modern Order: A History of the American People and their Institutions, 1917–1933 (New York: St. Martin's Press, 1979); and Brian Balogh, "Reorganizing the Organizational Synthesis: Federal-Professional Relations in Modern America," *Studies in American Political Development* 5, no. 1 (spring 1991): 119–72.

For the same reasons that the urban institutional financial historians proved helpful in providing a theoretical basis for state-centered causality, I also have found Elisabeth S. Clemens, *The People's Lobby: Organizational Innovation and the Rise of Interest Group Politics in the United States, 1890–1925* (Chicago: University of Chicago Press, 1997), quite helpful in conceptualizing political changes during this period. I also found the essays in Sidney M. Milkis and Jerome M. Mileur, eds., *Progressivism and the New Democracy* (Amherst: University of Massachusetts Press, 1999), ultimately more useful than Elizabeth Sanders, *Roots of Reform: Farmers, Workers, and the American State, 1877–1917* (Chicago: University of Chicago Press, 1999), simply because the latter focused more on national events, whereas the former looked at other levels of government as well.

Finally, for historical and theoretical justification for studying state government in particular, I am indebted to James Bryce, *The American Commonwealth*, 3rd ed., 2 vols. (New York: Macmillan, 1906); Ballard C. Campbell, *Representative Democracy: Public Policy and Midwestern Legislatures in the Late Nineteenth Century* (Cambridge, Mass.: Harvard University Press, 1980); and William R. Brock, *Investigation and Responsibility: Public Responsibility in the United States, 1865–1900* (New York: Cambridge University Press, 1984).

INDEX